Leading Decisively!
Leading Faithfully!
Reflections and Markers

Edward LeBron Fairbanks

Published in association with
BoardServe LLC, Lakeland, Florida 33811

For information regarding bulk purchases of this book,
please e-mail the author at: lfairbanks@boardserve.org.

See additional resources at: www.boardserve.org.

Library of Congress Cataloging-in-Publication Data

Boardserve LLC
ISBN-13: 978-0692780169

Leading Decisively!
Leading Faithfully!
Reflections and Markers

Edward LeBron Fairbanks
BoardServe LLC Founder and Director

Education Commissioner
Church of the Nazarene, retired

President Emeritus
Mount Vernon Nazarene University
Asia-Pacific Nazarene Theological Seminary

Foreword by Dr. Jesse Middendorf
General Superintendent Emeritus, Church of the Nazarene
Executive Director, Center for Pastoral Leadership
Nazarene Theological Seminary

Dedication

To Anne, the love of my life for 50 plus years! You love me, pray for and support me as together we continue to minister in various countries around the world. Your love for Christ and daily walk with Him models a maturing Christian who is "being transformed into the likeness of Christ" (II Corinthians 3:18). Your listening ear, warm heart and wise counsel bless individuals whom you encounter and mentor. Your patience with me is pure grace. Your quiet and gentle spirit profoundly impacts me! I love you and am grateful for you.

To Stephen, this book is a love gift to you. You are an ardent supporter and fierce defender of me as I have attempted to lead decisively with clear vision, deep humility, and intense resolve. If, for no other reason than to meaningfully pass on to you what has been so bountifully passed to me through education, experiences, relationships and assignments, then this writing task was worth the effort. Please take this gift, make the thoughts your own, and pass them to others as you attempt to integrate the faith you confess on Sunday to the way you live and lead throughout the week!

Acknowledgments

Dr. Sheila J. Clyburn, associate professor of education and academic affairs editor at Lincoln Memorial University, Harrogate, Tennessee, served as editor for this book. The text would not have been published without Dr. Clyburn's editing expertise!

Dr. Stan Toler, general superintendent emeritus, Church of the Nazarene, released the rights of the book we co-authored, *Learning to be Last*, published by Beacon Hill Press of Kansas City. Material found in our co-written book was included in this text. Dr. Toler has been and continues to be an encourager and inspiration to me. I am grateful for the transfer of all rights to me concerning the book.

Mr. Mark Brown, vice president of Nazarene Publishing House and Beacon Hill Press of Kansas City, provided a publication and copyright reversion letter for the book, *Learning to be Last*.

Grace Tia, Ernalyn Fausto, Ervz Tia, and other members of the incredibly talented team of WM Communications Asia-Pacific prepared the graphics and the layout of this book. WMC-AP is located at Asia-Pacific Nazarene Theological Seminary, Manila, Philippines (www.wmc-ap.org).

It was also a delight and privilege to work with Mrs. Bonnie Perry, book editor for Beacon Hill Press of Kansas City.

Appreciation

To the Regional Education Coordinators (2017) for the Church of the Nazarene. These individuals continue to inspire me as they seek to strengthen the educational institutions on the regions they serve. They work tirelessly and strategically, often behind the scenes, with school leaders and boards on their regions and collaboratively through the International Course of Study Advisory Committee and the International Board of Education. They are my friends and heroes:

Rev. Gabriel Benjiman
Africa Region. Johannesburg, South Africa

Dr. John E. Moore
Asia-Pacific Region. Singapore, Singapore

Rev. Stéphane Tibi
Eurasia Region. Büsingen, Germany

Dr. Rubén E. Fernández
Mesoamerica Region. Panama City, Panama

Dr. Jorge L. Julca
South America Region. Buenos Aires, Argentina

Dr. Dean G. Blevins
USA/Canada Region. Lenexa, Kansas, USA

Table of Contents

Compassion: Enabling Others to See What They Have
Not Seen in Themselves
Endurance: Staying with the Assignment
God Has Given To You

Foreword

Leadership theorists are everywhere. Books on leadership abound. The hunger for knowledge, skill, and effectiveness in leadership is evident in the overwhelming number of new university degrees, seminary centers, and leadership conferences that vie for the attention of all of us.

But effective and fruitful leadership as a demonstrated way of living is in short supply. Where we find it, we need to pay attention.

I have known Dr. LeBron Fairbanks for over half a century. We were students together in college and seminary and have frequently been colleagues in ministry and leadership settings in these fifty plus years. Leadership was not his pursuit. It was simply the means by which he worked. He led by being.

His leadership has been demonstrated in local church ministry, global mission settings, and in educational institutions. As an educator, he was effective in the classroom and as a department head. He served on the staff of European Nazarene College and as president of Asia-Pacific Nazarene Theological Seminary. His longest tenure of service was as president of Mount Vernon Nazarene University. He later served as leader of the International Board of Education and as Commissioner of Education for the Church of the Nazarene.

What some have worked hard to learn, LeBron lived innately. But he also studied carefully, read widely, and learned from some of the best leaders in the world.

Even in retirement, LeBron has given himself to teaching leadership skills and practices to both secular and religious institutions. He has worked with boards of trustees, CEOs, pastors, university presidents, and a wide range of other leadership settings. His goal is to develop leaders who are capable of transforming their ministries or institutions for fruitful and effective fulfillment of their mission.

In this book is the distilled wisdom of decades of effective leadership. This is not mere theory. This is a vision for leadership that reflects a life of selfless service and vision. While there are practices and skills that are absolutely essential in the work of leadership in Christian ministry, behind the skills and practices is the foundation of spiritual maturity and reflective thinking. Here is hope and help for Christian leaders in the confusing and sometimes frightening environment in which we find ourselves today. The world is rapidly changing. Christian leaders need help that is timeless and true. I believe you will find this resource one of the most helpful.

I have shelves crammed with books on leadership, written by many widely respected leaders. I have learned much from them and treasure especially those books and authors who have shaped my thinking and my practice in ways that have made me a better ministry leader than I would have been without their help.

This is one of those books that I believe will find a valued place in the hands of every leader, whatever the level of responsibility. This is wisdom, borne of fruitfulness and demonstrated in a life of effective service in leadership.

I found myself resonating deeply with the Six Markers for Decisive Leadership. They should be carefully poured over, studied, and pondered. Their implementation will take prayerful, intentional discipline. Their effectiveness will require constant engagement with those with whom the leader is called to work. They cannot be "administered" unilaterally. They will require a selflessness that does not seek prominence. They will demand a spiritual sensitivity that is willing to rely on the Holy Spirit for direction.

This book could well last for the next fifty years as a vital tool for Christian ministry. Its truth is timeless, and its approach engaging. I commend it to you as a resource you will grow to treasure.

Jesse C. Middendorf, DMin.
General Superintendent Emeritus, Church of the Nazarene
Executive Director, Center for Pastoral Leadership
Nazarene Theological Seminary

Your attitude should be the same as that of Jesus Christ:
Who, being in the very nature God, did not consider equality
with God something to be grasped, but made himself nothing,
taking the very nature of a servant, being made in human likeness. And
being found in appearance as a man, he humbled himself and became
obedient to death even death on a cross!
Philippians 2:5-8 (NIV)

The servant leader is a servant first... It begins with the natural
feeling that one wants to serve, to serve first. Then conscious choice
brings one to aspire to lead... The difference manifests itself
in the care taken by the servant-first to make sure that
other people's highest priority needs are being served.
Robert Greenleaf, *Servant Leadership* (p. 13)

If anyone wants to be first, he must be the very last,
and the servant of all.
Mark 9:35 (NIV)

You know that those who are regarded as rulers of the Gentiles lord it
over them, and their high officials exercise authority over them. Not so
with you. Instead, whoever wants to become great among you must be
your servant, and, whoever wants to be first must be slave to all. For
even the Son of Man did not come to be served, but to serve, and to give
his life a ransom for many.
Mark 10:42-44 (NIV)

Preface

This book is intended to serve as a multi-lingual, cross-cultural, and baccalaureate-level text on leading decisively and faithfully in Christian communities. It reflects convictions to which I remain captive, as I live and lead as a maturing disciple of Jesus Christ.

Following my retirement as president of Mount Vernon Nazarene University in Mount Vernon, Ohio, I was elected to the position of education commissioner for the Church of the Nazarene. As the education commissioner, it was my delight and privilege to work closely with the International Board of Education (IBOE), a Board representing Nazarene institutions globally, the denomination's regional education coordinators from the Asia-Pacific, Eurasia, South America, Mesoamerica, Africa, USA/Canada regions, and many of the administrators and board leaders of the education institutions of the Church of the Nazarene.

The denomination, as of 2015, had 52 colleges, universities, and seminaries on campuses and learning centers in 118 nations, with resources linked together in a network of support and collaboration under the IBOE. Over 50,000 students were enrolled in these institutions at that time, with many of these adults preparing for Christian service.

My commitment to students enrolled in these institutions began in 1978, when I joined the European Nazarene College faculty in Büsingen, Germany, as academic dean. My interest increased as I worked in various assignments at Southern Nazarene University in Bethany, Oklahoma; Asia-Pacific Nazarene Theological Seminary in Manila, Philippines; and Mount Vernon

During these years of higher education administration, I continued to return to classrooms in our educational institutions in various countries. I enjoyed teaching courses related to Christian leadership and found responsiveness to the structure and content of the classes. I also discovered that a need existed for an undergraduate-level text across the regions to prepare adults for ministry.

At the encouragement of several of the regional education coordinators with whom I worked, this book began to take shape. Hopefully and prayerfully, the following pages will address this leadership challenge in Christian communities.

Introduction

So you are asked to assume a leadership role within a Christian faith community. A Sunday school teacher or leader is needed for a small group Bible study, and you have accepted the request to lead the group. A congregation has called you to *pastor* their local church, while you are working full-time in other employment. You were elected to a position of leadership on the church board, in the choir, on a committee, or to be the *head* usher.

Perhaps, you were selected to lead a community not-for-profit organization for the homeless or an after- school mentoring program for children and teens. You may have been elected to the community association board where you live.

A cross-cultural assignment may have taken you out of your comfort zone and the familiar, and you are experiencing behavior within the group that challenges you. You do not feel qualified for the leadership assignment. In fact, you recommended others for the very position you have been asked to assume. Yet, when asked, and following prayer about the request, you felt an inward *nudge* to accept.

If any of these scenarios are true, you may find this book beneficial as you lead within your faith community or even outside the structures of the church where you live and work. Techniques for leading are not offered, nor are *easy steps* outlined. Rather, a perspective is given; and reflections are shared, along with a theological vision for leading others. Summarized are the values, priorities, and principles that have guided me in leading others in numerous countries and diverse assignments. Perhaps the "driving forces" outlined in the book can serve to motivate you in your work with others. These convictions continue

1

to characterize me at my best and challenge me at my worst, as I strive to be an effective Christian servantleader.

As much as leaders, like you and me, want to be known as decisive, with our decision-making marked by firmness and our action characterized by certainty and conclusiveness, even more critical in leading others is a distinctively Christian quality and depth of communication. Caring for others is the mark of greatness, more so than decisiveness. Our testimony of faith in Jesus Christ must increasingly inform and transform the way we live in and lead a faith community, as that community is expressed in the home, on the job, in discipleship class, youth group, church board, local congregation, or seminary. The *Sermon on the Mount* — not the latest relevant leadership text — must shape us as we lead our Christian community of faith.

Three compelling convictions prod us as we explore our vocational calling to lead decisively, with a vision to serve: convictions about who we are as the people of God; what we are called to do in the mission of God; and how we live together as the family of God. These three cornerstones — a **vision** about our identity, a **passion** about our calling or vocation, and an **obsession** about the faith community — are common threads that grow stronger in the life of decisive leaders with a vision to serve.

As I was thinking about this book, I realized that to *lead decisively and to lead faithfully,* we need to expand the three cornerstones into markers that guide our behavior as leaders. Indeed, they serve as boundaries and perimeters. For many of us, embracing these six markers will constitute change in how we approach the task of leading others.

If leaders are to assist "the led" to think and act Christianly, we must wholeheartedly embrace these decisive servant *markers* and major ideas around which this book is written:

1. The PASSION for leading decisively is grounded in a vision of ministry.

2. The IMPERATIVE in leading decisively is speaking to, not past, each other.

3. The GOAL of leading decisively is focused on effectively preparing the Body of Christ — the People of God — for mission and ministry.

4. The METHOD of leading decisively in accomplishing the vision includes mentoring, diligent board governance, missional planning, and a robust community.

5. The PAIN of leading decisively is experienced in the tension between good and godly people over vision, values, and traditions.

6. The EVIDENCE of leading decisively is reflected in the qualitative growth of the led, individually and collectively.

There must be a vision within the Christian community regarding ministry that is shared by both the leader and the led. Without this shared vision of ministry, the community of faith will experience disintegration and despair. Conversely, mobilizing a Christian community for ministry hinges on a radical commitment to our identity as:

- brothers and sisters in Christ, fellow travelers on a spiritual journey;

- members together of Christ's body, a fellowship of God's people;

- a microcosm of the kingdom of God on earth, a community of faith; and

- a sacramental community in and through which the grace of God flows.

The vision for this book is that a younger generation of leaders will embrace the biblical model of "servant" as the driving force and organizing principle as they seek to lead decisively. A deep sense of stewardship compels me to pass on to others what has been so freely given to me, and in a way that they *"will also be qualified to teach others"* (cf II Timothy 2:2).

In the context of biblical and theological foundations and from the perspective of spiritual, strategic, and skills formation, readers are invited to a lifelong, passionate pursuit of and an unswerving, intense commitment to a distinctively Christian identity in leading others. There is, indeed, a profound Presence and motivation, or a disconcerting disconnection, between the Christian faith we profess on Sunday and the way we lead decisively throughout the week within a community of faith.

Fundamentally, I believe, leading decisively is grounded in biblical perspective and not in organizational skills. It means that the primary motivation of our actions is deeply theological. The Spirit of God within us enables us to make decisions grounded in our identity and life in Christ and our biblical worldview. Skills, of course, are needed. However, sharp skills without Christian motives easily lead to manipulation. Join with me as we further

4

explore the concepts that are inherent in the Christian servant leader who is not afraid to lead decisively. They will characterize us at our best and convict us at our worst.

You know that those who are regarded as rulers of the Gentiles lord it over them, and their high officials exercise authority over them. Not so with you, Instead, whoever wants to become great among you must be your servant, and whoever wants to be first must be slave to all among you (Mark 10:42-43 NIV).

"Brother [sister] let me be your servant..." (*Sing to the Lord*, 1993, p. 679), as we reflect and explore together what it means to lead decisively...with clear vision, deep humility, and an intense resolve to serve others.

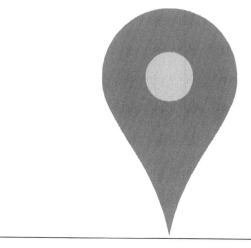

MARKER ONE:

THE *PASSION* FOR LEADING DECISIVELY IS GROUNDED IN A *VISION* OF MINISTRY.

Chapter 1

MARKER ONE:
THE PASSION FOR LEADING DECISIVELY
IS GROUNDED IN A *VISION* OF MINISTRY.

Christian ministry is the extension of the service of Jesus in our world, incarnating the healing, guiding, sustaining, reconciling work of Jesus in the lives of those with whom we work and live.

Edward LeBron Fairbanks

The first marker to be discussed probes the foundations of leading spiritually with particular attention given to a biblical understanding of ministry within a Christian community. How is leading decisively and faithfully expressed in a Christian community? Why must a "theological vision" of those with whom we live and work precede "organizational vision?"

A Vision of Ministry

A vision is a consuming, fervent, and compelling inner picture. It is seeing what others do not see. At the very heart of a servant leader is a theological vision of our identity within the Christian fellowship. First and foremost, both the leader and the led are the graced, blessed, called, and gifted People of God. And those, with whom we work, on the basis of their testimony of faith, are the "Body of Christ and the Fellowship of the Spirit" (Ephesians 3:6; Acts 2:42).

How do we "envision" the people with whom we work in our present ministry assignment? Do we have a consuming, passionate, compelling inner picture   (vision)

8

of (a) who we are as the People of God; (b) how they may live together as the Family of God; and (c) what they are called to do with their lives in the Mission of God?

Only after we answer these questions are we prepared to begin equipping individuals for their ministry to each other and their mission in the world. This requires a vision shaped by scripture!

What is Ministry?

In its briefest and most general understanding, ministry is "diakonia" or SERVICE. At its very best, ministry is passionate service to others in Jesus' name. Certain words help us understand the various dimensions of Christian ministry — words like caring, sharing, growing, relating, teaching, and even confronting. Ministry in the New Testament perspective takes the form of holding the hand of a person engulfed in fear, listening intently to a person in trouble, crying with a person who is hurting, or embracing the individual who is grieving. It may include taking students or parishioners to the store for groceries or confronting in love their lack of discipline or careless habits. Ministry encompasses the sharing of the Christian faith or a verse of scripture with another in time of need. Christ in His ministry pursued all these and more with a passion beyond our understanding.

Christian ministry is the extension of the service of Jesus in our world, incarnating the healing, guiding, sustaining, reconciling work of Jesus in the lives of those with whom we work and live. If you are a Christian, you are called to Christian ministry.

Ministry understood in this broadest sense is the context for our specific ministry. We may be called and

9

gifted for pastoral ministry, teaching ministry, evangelism ministry, music ministry, or leadership ministry. It is futile and self-defeating to seek to function within our personal calling, while ignoring the broader mandate to serve others in Jesus' name.

Jesus defined success in Christian ministry in terms of service or self-giving to others in the name and place of God (Matthew 25:34-46). Our responsibility as leaders is to care for God's people as a compassionate shepherd cares for his sheep, leading and teaching them in the ways of God. Our leadership mandate is to motivate, equip, and enable the People of God to develop their gifts and give their lives in meaningful service to others in Jesus' name. Our ministry is helping others prepare for their ministries.

Dietrich Bonhoeffer (1954) in *Life Together: The Classic Exploration of Faith in Community* listed seven expressions of ministry (pp. 90-109) by which a Christian community must be judged and characterized.

1. **The Ministry of Holding One's Tongue**
    "He who holds his tongue in check controls both mind and body," James tells us. "Do not let any unwholesome talk come out of your mouth..." is an admonishment from the Ephesian epistle. When this passage characterizes us, we will be able to cease from constantly criticizing the other person, judging him and condemning him, putting him in his particular place. We can allow the other to exist as a completely free person.

2. **The Ministry of Meekness**
    This is "caring more for others than for self." "Do not think of yourself more highly than you ought," Paul tells us in Romans 12:3. John tells us to make no effort to obtain the praise that comes only from God. He

who serves must learn to think first of others.

3. **The Ministry of Listening**
   The first service that one owes to others in the fellowship consists of listening. Listening can be a greater service to people than speaking.

4. **The Ministry of Active Helpfulness**
   Simply assist others within the Christian community in external matters, big and small.

5. **The Ministry of Bearing (Supporting)**
   "Carry each other's burden" is the challenge of Galatians 6:2. Bearing means forbearing and sustaining one another in love. Ephesians 4:2 commands us to *"be humble and gentle; be patient, bearing with one another in love."*

6. **The Ministry of Proclaiming**
   This is the ministry of the word of God. Bonhoeffer (1954) does not mean the message of Scripture proclaimed in a formal setting such as in the worship service. He is referring to the free communication of the word of God from person to person. He is referring to that unique situation in which one person becomes a witness in human words to another, with Christian consolation.

7. **The Ministry of Authority (Leadership)**
   Jesus states in Mark 10:43, "Whosoever wants to be great among you must be first your servant, and whoever wants to be first must be your slave." This is the paradox of ministry. Jesus made authority in the fellowship dependent upon brotherly service (p. 108).

For Bonhoeffer (1954), these practical expressions of Christian ministry provide the *context* within which our specific ministries must function. This is particularly true as it relates to the specific ministry of leadership.

The ministry of Christ reveals three salient features:

1. Christ — the Servant. His ministry was a *servant* ministry. *"If anyone wants to be first, he must be the very last, and the servant of all"* Mark 9:35. He demonstrated His service to His Father by doing the will of Him who sent Him, and to the people by accepting them as they were and meeting their needs, whether by healing the sick, feeding the hungry, or simply by making time to listen and be with the sinner, the outcast, or the disregarded member of society.

2. Christ — the Teacher. His ministry involved *teaching*. He taught with authority. He was known as "Rabbi, teacher." The proclamation of the gospel, the announcement of the kingdom to all who had ears to hear was conducted not only in word but also in deed. It was clear teaching, adapted to the needs of the listeners, and delivered in easy-to-understand illustrations and examples.

3. Christ — the Sacrifice. He was the Lamb of God, who takes away the sin of the world by His sacrifice on the cross. He laid down His life by His own free will in obedience to His Father. His ministry was essentially *sacrificial and priestly.*

If all Christians are called to be extensions of Christ, then the ministry of the People of God will be characterized by service, teaching, and sacrifice to the people with whom we come in contact.

Decisive Servants and the Led

How, then, can *our* ministry of Christian leadership enable *others* to fulfill *their* ministry to each other and *their* mission in the world? Leadership, for ministers of Christ, is known by the personalities it enriches, not by those it dominates or captivates. Are the people being served *growing* as Christians? Are they, themselves, becoming servants? These are crucial concerns for the leadership of God's people.

Robert Greenleaf (1977), in his outstanding book, *Servant Leadership: A Journey into the Nature of Legitimate Power*, suggests a thesis that those who are leaders must serve those whom they lead. Only those who serve, he believes, are fit for leadership (p. 10). Although written for the secular audience, the book contains many thoughts on servant leadership similar to the words of Jesus.

The late Dr. Harold Reed (1982), former president of Olivet Nazarene University and The Reed Institute for the Advanced Study of Leadership and author of the book, *The Dynamics of Leadership: Open the Door to Your Leadership Potential*, stated, "The quality of your leadership is largely determined by your philosophy of life" (p. 23). If our philosophy of life is based on a biblical theology of church and ministry, then how we lead, or our style of leadership, will focus on the qualitative growth of the led as ministers of Jesus Christ, called to serve others in His name.

Understood this way, Christian ministry is a *shared ministry* with every believer serving and supporting one another, using Spirit-given gifts to stimulate personal and corporate growth and reconciliation in both the church and the world. Ministry, like missions, is a function and expression of the whole church. It is not something that only a few persons are called, trained, and ordained to do — but a function of the People of God.

13

A Model of Ministry

Perhaps, the following outline of my model of ministry (Figure 1.1) will summarize this discussion on ministry. It attempts to conceptualize the relationship of the leadership ministry of the pastor-teacher to the ministry of the People of God whom s/he serves.

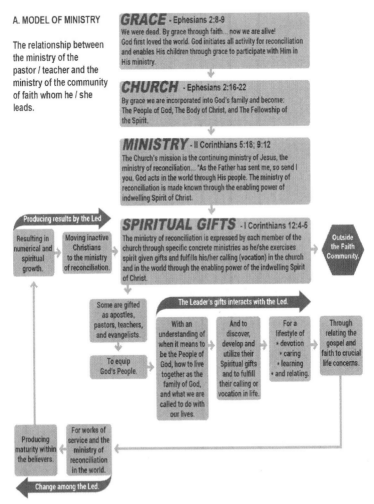

Figure 1.1. Model of ministry. © E.L. Fairbanks

14

Notice the sequence from GRACE—we were dead (Ephesians 2:1), and now we are alive by GRACE through faith (Ephesians 2:8). God initiates and enables His children through GRACE to participate with Him in His Mission.

Following Figure 1.1 full circle from Grace through the Leader interacting with the Led, through Change among the Led, finally through Producing Results by the Led, it becomes clear our ministry of leadership is to prepare others for their ministries. Do you notice how the Led then begin to be integrated into the "Ministry" portion of the sequence of events?

GRACE incorporates us into the CHURCH, God's family, to become the People of God, The Body of Christ, and the Fellowship of the Spirit (Ephesians 2:19-22).

The Mission of the CHURCH is the continuing MINISTRY of Jesus, the ministry of reconciliation (II Corinthians 5:18; 9:12). *"As the Father has sent me,"* Jesus said, *"so I am sending you"* (John 20:21 NLT). God acts in the world through His people.

Each member of the CHURCH through specific, concrete SPIRITUAL GIFTS expresses the MINISTRY of reconciliation. GRACE accomplishes this as s/he fulfills her/his calling or vocation in the church and in the world, through the enabling power of the indwelling Spirit of Christ (I Cor. 12:4-5, 11).

Some are gifted as "apostles, pastors, teachers, and evangelists" to equip, prepare, and shape God's People for their ministry (Ephesians 4:11-16).

These leadership gifts interact with the led with "grace-gifts" to equip God's People with an understanding of what it means to be the People of God, how to live together as the family of God, and what we are called to do with our lives in the mission of God. God's People are prepared to discover, develop, and utilize their spiritual gifts and to fulfill their calling or vocation in life (Romans 12:6-8). They are prepared for a lifestyle of devotion, caring, learning, and relating the gospel and faith to crucial life concerns.

The equipping of God's People prepares God's People for "works of service" (Ephesians 4:12) and the ministry of reconciliation (II Corinthians 5:17-20). Christians are equipped in their faith, resulting in spiritual growth and Christian maturity. Even passive Christians increasingly participate in the ministry of reconciliation, as these believers exercise spiritual gifts in their calling or vocation where they live, work, and serve outside the faith community.

The "shared vision" of ministry. Shared vision and Christian leadership are very closely intertwined, since the led are to be served by the leader, who shares the vision with the led. Again, fundamental for the Christian leader is not so much "organizational vision" but "theological vision."

The late Henri Nouwen (1979), in his book, *Clowning in Rome: Reflections on Solitude, Celibacy, Prayer and Contemplation,* reflected on a sculptor who worked hard with his hammer and chisel on a large block of marble. He continued,

A little boy who was watching him saw nothing more than large and small pieces of stone falling away left and right. He had no idea what was happening. But when the boy returned to the studio a few weeks later, he saw to his surprise a large, powerful lion sitting in the place where the marble had stood. With great excitement the boy ran to the sculptor and said, "Sir, tell me, how did you know there was a lion in the marble?" (pp. 83-84)

16

What do we *see* in the people with whom we work? Do we see problems or possibilities? The present situation or the future potential? Our challenge is to see beyond the past, or even the present with its problems, to "dream" or "see" redeemed individuals — all of whom are called to live as an extension of Jesus in their world, incarnating the healing, sustaining, reconciling work of Jesus in the lives of those with whom they work and live.

As leaders, we need a consuming, passionate, compelling inner picture of (a) *who* we are as the People of God; (b) *how* we may live together as the family of God; and (c) *what* we are called to do with our lives in the mission of God.

Leadership - The t*ransference* of vision. We must transfer our vision of ministry to those for whom we have Christian care and responsibility; and they will, in turn, transfer their vision to others! To believe that all Christians, even those with whom we work and who sometimes make life so difficult, are called and gifted for the ministry of Christ is humbling, frustrating, demanding, and necessary! More and more, we need to see ourselves as equippers of ministers. Unfortunately, most of us have been educated to be ministers, not to be enablers of ministers.

Shared ministry demands deep *seeing* and deep *visioning*. Only the person who can see the invisible can do the impossible. Questions such as What if...? and Why not...? ought to permeate our mindset regarding the Christians with whom we work. What if...they were all called to the Christian ministry? Why not...assume it is true and proceed accordingly?

The late Quaker philosopher, Dr. Eldon Trueblood (1952), stated in his book, *Your Other Vocation,* "If, in the average church we should suddenly take seriously that every lay member, man and woman, is really a minister of Christ, we could have something of a revolution..." (p. 167).

Trueblood (1952) continued, "Originally, in the New Testament, the term 'laity' meant all the people in the early Christian movement, the *laos*, but finally a layperson has come to mean any nonprofessional whatever the field under consideration" (p. 35).

He believed that "whatever person's ordinary vocation in the world, ...the ministry can be his *other* vocation and perhaps his truest vocation" (p. 46). Laypersons, he believed, "are not assistants" (p. 46) to the pastor, to help him do his work. Rather, the pastor is to be their assistant. His function is "to help the members for the work of ministry" (p. 46), to which God has called them.

Only from this perspective will ministry be mutually understood and shared. Without this shared vision, ministry in and through the local church or theological institution is as impossible as a triangle with two sides. Ministry happens when the pastor and the congregation, administrator and students, leader and led have a vision of Christian ministry and pursue it together. The more consuming the vision, the greater the commitment to ministry.

"We must be captured by a vision, which transcends ministry *to* the people, and ministry *for* the people, to ministry *with* the people and ministry *by* the people" (Kinsler, 1983, p. 1). The shared vision of ministry demands a *passionate conviction* regarding ministry that sets out to do something about the insight. Our leadership ministry is helping others understand and develop their ministry. When those with similar vision are drawn together, something extraordinary occurs.

18

HOW, THEN, CAN WE COMMUNICATE A VISION OF MINISTRY THAT WILL BECOME A SHARED VISION?

Jesus challenges us in Luke 6:40, *"When a student is fully trained, he will become like his teacher"* (or his pastor or school president)! Ministry is always incarnated and enfleshed. Ministry must be lived out! But what is it about ourselves that we want our students, staff, or parishioners to catch from us?

We want our people to catch from us a servant spirit, committed to *motivating, equipping,* and *enabling them to serve others in Jesus' name.* We want to pass on our passion and vision, so, in turn, they enter into the ministry cycle. This is success for the Christian leader! This is what it means to be a servant leader!

What we are confronted with is a need to communicate a lifestyle that is distinctly Christian and self-giving at the core. How do you teach commitments, priorities, values, and spiritual disciplines? How do you teach a lifestyle?

"Follow me as I follow Christ," I Corinthians 11:1. *"You ought to follow my example,"* II Thessalonians 3:7. *"Put into practice what you have learned, received or heard from me or seen in me,"* Philippians 4:9. *"We did this in order to make ourselves a model for you to follow,"* Paul states in II Thessalonians 3:9. The Apostle gave these words to the Christians under his care with humility; we must do the same for those for whom we are responsible.

For Paul, a key way to "teach a lifestyle" was through personal example. What leadership qualities must others see in us as organizational or institutional leaders, teachers, or pastors, if we are to transfer our vision of ministry effectively? Ephesians 4:25-32 provides for a servant leadership lifestyle (see Marker Two for an elaboration of this lifestyle).

19

Ephesians 4 begins with the challenge to walk worthy of our calling as Christians. The characteristics of the person "walking worthy" follow the challenge. We are instructed to be gentle, humble, patient, and supportive of each other. In so living, we will "maintain the unity of the spirit in the bond of peace."

Paul is not so much talking about administrative techniques but Christian attitudes underlying our actions and activities. We are co-laborers together in the body of Christ (Ephesians 4:25). We function with others out of an "I-Thou" frame of reference. The people with whom we work are God's own creation.

Leading others decisively from a distinctively biblical and theological perspective is our goal! These convictional principles and concepts may not be found in the latest secular textbook on leadership; but they are foundational for the leaders who want their people to catch from them a servant spirit, committed to preparing them to serve others in Jesus' name.

Our assignment, then, as leaders who are Christian, is greater and more demanding than communicating facts, dates, persons, places, or events. Our responsibility includes a passionate servant Christian lifestyle that motivates and equips the led to *serve others in Jesus' name.*

If this is our *vision* of ministry and our leadership lifestyle is characterized by Ephesians 4:25-32, then those whom we serve and for whom we are responsible will increasingly adopt this vision as their vision of ministry. They will not see in us a finished product. Rather, they will discover in us an on-going process of transformation into Christ-likeness.

20

It is not easy. As a university president, I continually asked, "What does it mean to be a servant to my students, faculty and staff, parents, pastors, and community and denominational leaders? What does it mean to be a servant in the midst of *all* the expectations, roles, and functions?"

I well remember a faculty member, after signing a contract to teach for the following year, informed me rather rudely that he was resigning and going to another university to teach. I could have insisted on his fulfilling the contract but realized that I should agree to the breach of contract. Within several weeks of his departure from the university, I received what I felt was a "blistering" letter from him, outlining complaints and problems he had with the university and with me. I purposely delayed responding to him for several days. Instead of trying to answer his points one by one, I wrote to him a letter of apology for apparently failing him, while he was on our faculty. I asked him for his forgiveness. I did not receive a response from him.

What about the risks of believing in others? Misunderstandings? Abuses? Betrayals? Pain? Hurts? Is it worth it? Is it really worth the risk of being a servant leader?

I am growing in my understanding of the profoundness of these questions and their answers. Slowly, but with inner confidence, I am developing a deep conviction — theologically grounded — that I must accept the risks and serve my people with integrity, if I am to be a Christian leader. And you, too, will be challenged to find such responses in the situations you face. Some will hurt us; but we must not withdraw from the many who respond to our trust, encouragement, mentoring, and confidence we place in them.

21

The temptation for us as leaders is to withdraw from people when we have been hurt or misunderstood. It is true, I believe, that some individuals may abuse a close relationship with their leader. We need to remember that even Jesus had His Judas. From my perspective, however, the large majority of those we lead will respond to encouragement, guidance, mentoring, and up-building.

Definitions of Leadership

Literature abounds with definitions of leadership. Christian leadership is, *I believe, humble service to others for the purpose of enabling them, through example and teaching, to live their lives under the Lordship of Christ and to understand, accept, and fulfill their ministry to each other and their mission in the world.*

The late Dr. Harold Reed (1982), long-time president of Olivet Nazarene College, in his book, The *Dynamics of Leadership: Open the Door to Your Leadership Potential,* stated:

Leadership is known by the personalities it enriches, not by those it dominates or captivates. Leadership is not a process of exploitation of others for extraneous ends. It is a process of helping others to discover themselves in the achieving of aims that have become intrusive to them. (p. 7)

In a national conference for presidents of Christian colleges and universities (CCCU), Max de Pree stated, "The first responsibility of leadership is to define reality" (Max De Pree, n.d.).

Peter Koestenbaum (2002) stated, "Leadership is the art of combining results and heart," (p. 177).

What is your response to these definitions? What are the key words, phrases, or key themes in the statements? How would you modify the references? Take a moment and reflect on various definitions of leadership with which you are familiar, and then reflect on these questions:

1. Which is the most meaningful definition of leadership to you? Why?

2. What are some recurring themes in the definitions of leadership?

3. How would you combine your thoughts on leading others with the thrust of this first marker of leading decisively being grounded in a vision of ministry? Write down your emerging thoughts below:

_____

_____

How clearly we "see" this vision will determine the degree to which our leadership will be judged "successful" in biblical perspective. In the Christian community, leading decisively and ministry effectiveness of the led are almost synonymous.

Spend some time reflecting on the following scriptures as you shape your definition of Christian leadership:

Romans 12:1-3, 9-13   II Corinthians 8-10
Philippians 2:5-11   Galatians 3:26-28
I Thessalonians 1, 2   Ephesians 5:15-21
I Corinthians 2   Galatians 5:16-26
I Corinthians 12-13   II Corinthians 4:1-11
II Corinthians 5:15-25

Add additional scriptural passages that you find helpful in understanding your role of leadership in the faith community.

Five Important Lessons

Over the years, I have learned five practical lessons on accepting those whom we lead who do not necessarily embrace the vision of ministry outlined in this chapter.

1. Good and godly people differ and sometimes collide with the leader.

2. Many issues over which we experience conflict are culturally, ethnically, local community and family-based matters, and not a violation of scripture.

3. Differences that divide us have the power to alienate members of the body of Christ and to impact the work of God negatively in our communities.

4. Respecting those who differ with us is to love them, as God loves them.

5. Acceptance of others implies that we can learn from them.

Please add lessons you have learned regarding good and godly people who differ with you regarding your vision of ministry.

1.
2.
3.

Lead decisively and lead faithfully with a *vision to serve* and with a commitment to equip servant leaders! If you and I are captured by this vision of ministry formation and are characterized by a servant leadership lifestyle, then the groups we lead — regardless of their sizes — will be life-giving, growth-producing, and *distinctly Christian*.

Find a way to serve your people. The cycle of Christian ministry will empower the people you lead to reach out and serve others in Jesus' name! *This* is servant leadership! To *this* ministry, we are called.

Whatever else our assignment involves, the responsibility of leading others compels us to live a servant lifestyle that motivates those whom we lead to serve others in Jesus' name. Our responsibility in ministry is to internalize the passion of grace, making it part of how we lead (our leadership lifestyle), so it passes to those we lead; and they make it part of their leadership lifestyle. Watching the cycle of Christian leadership unfold and come to fruition in those we lead is the reward of ministry.

In Chapter One, we connected the passion of servant leaders to a biblical vision of ministry. Christian leadership begins with a prayer and passion for reflecting Christ's love for others. Step one for decisive leaders is to envision Christ's passion to serve and to transfer this vision to those we lead.

Mobilizing a Christian community for ministry hinges on a wholehearted commitment to our identity within the faith community as the People of God, The Body of Christ, and the Fellowship of the Spirit. This *vision* within the Christian community regarding ministry impacts both pastor and laity.

With a laser-beam focus, the orientation and motivation of servant leaders must be grounded resolutely in a biblical vision of *ministry*.

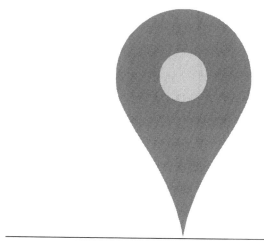

MARKER TWO:

THE IMPERATIVE IN LEADING DECISIVELY IS SPEAKING TO, NOT PAST, EACH OTHER.

Chapter Two

MARKER TWO: THE IMPERATIVE IN LEADING DECISIVELY IS SPEAKING TO, NOT PAST, EACH OTHER.

"Do not let any unwholesome talk come out of your mouths, but only what is helpful for building others up according to their needs, that it may benefit those who listen."

Ephesians 4:29

Satir (1976) believed that "communication is to relationships what breathing is to maintaining life..." (p. 20). To paraphrase Satir (1976), I have come to see that communication is to leading what breathing is to living.

I had a vivid dream one night while visiting friends in a nearby state. For some reason, I was in an inner city, somewhere in the United States. I was traveling with a friend, and the two of us had just witnessed a violent argument in a store. One man from the inner city was selling merchandise to another gentleman, who was not from the inner city.

I cannot remember the cause of the argument, but I remember the person from the inner city saying to the other individual, "You will never understand; you are not from here."

I remember listening very intently at both sides of the argument and believing parts of what each man was saying. The two people arguing finally separated. I remember being so moved by what I had just experienced that, for some reason, I had the courage to speak to the

28

man from the inner city. I said to him, "I really do not know who is right and who is wrong. I don't know what should be done in this situation." And then I continued, "What bothers me more is that what I have just experienced is a small picture of our society at large. We speak and argue vehemently from our perspective, always assuming that we are right." But what jolted me out of my dream was a statement I made to him with intense passion, "It seems like you were just talking past one another."

At that moment, I woke from my dream. Literally, my heart was pounding. I began to think about the dream and its implications. I couldn't get away from the words, "I really don't know who is right or wrong, but it seems like you were just talking past one another."

I began to ponder the implications of my dream for my own life and relationship with others. "I really don't know who is right or wrong, but it seems like we often just talk right past one another." *How often this /scenario is played out in real life a*nd how painful — even in our own Christian communities.

Questions for Decisive Leaders in a Faith Community

In the first year of teaching at the European Nazarene Bible College near Schaffhausen, Switzerland, I remember sharing a question in class: How can we live together, so that our relationships are redemptive and a witness to unbelievers of the reconciling work of Christ?

I soon realized that this is a leadership question relating to *vision* and to *communication*! How does my leading others enable them to fulfill their ministry to each other and their mission in the world in the context of a *dynamic laboratory* of learning how to live *together* as God's children? If, *"in Christ, all things are made new,"* (II Corinthians 5:17), then how does my testimony of faith in Christ transform the way I lead? What do we "see" in others who may differ with us over mission, vision, values, plans, and programs? Do we talk to them, or past them?

In the midst of conflicting expectations, multiple constituents, differing denominational backgrounds, various levels of maturity, multi-cultural perspectives, how can we live together Christianly? How does our pursuit of Christlikeness translate to a Christian leadership lifestyle?

For missionaries in cross-cultural situations, pastors in local churches, parents in homes, or ministry organization administrators working with volunteers, these questions become critical.

Often we are placed together, due to our leadership assignments, in a close community, in which we become aware of others' strengths and weaknesses. Our own personality differences soon become obvious. We realize that our specific leadership setting (as missionary, pastor, administrator, or parent) becomes a dynamic laboratory for learning how to live together as God's family. We realize how we respond to conflict under pressure.

The first three chapters of Ephesians are primarily indicative in the language structure and give statements of fact. They are doctrinal in nature and explain who we are in Christ. Chapters 4-6 of Ephesians are primarily imperative in nature and give commands of action, are ethically focused, and explain how we should live as Christians.

Ephesians 4:1 is the transition verse that invites us to walk worthy of our calling and to participate with God in His mission to reconcile the world unto Himself. Living the transformed life and participating in the reconciling mission and ministry of God is indeed a high and holy calling. How do we lead a faith community to understand and embrace this calling?

"Be completely humble and gentle; be patient; be supportive of one another in love. Make every effort to keep the unity of the Spirit in the bond of peace" (Ephesians 4: 2-3).

Paul states that reconciliation with God must be first demonstrated by living redemptively within the fellowship. In essence, the Apostle is saying, you will have credibility to tell non-Christians that they need to be reconciled to God, when grace-filled reconciliation is reflected within the fellowship of believers, particularly, in the way the group is led.

A Communication Model for Leading Decisively

"Speaking the truth in love..." (Ephesians 4:15a) is a powerful tool and biblical concept of Paul for leaders of Christian communities who daily seek to live the reconciled and transformed life. "Truth-telling in love" is an enabling principle for Christians to embrace and their leaders to model. However, the skill of *"making contact"* is not automatically developed when we are filled with God's Spirit.

Over the years, Figure 2.1 has provided me a model for thinking about the powerful and grace-enabled impact and doing the hard and necessary work of pastoral conversation in the communities of faith where I have served.

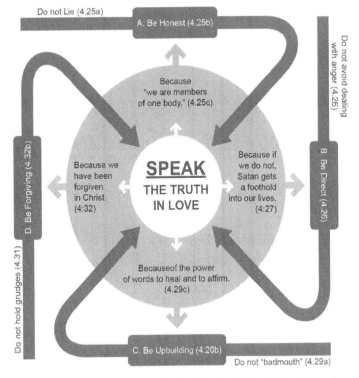

Figure 2.1. A communication model for leading decisively. © E.L. Fairbanks

Long ago, I told my students, *"I am captive to the relational convictions in the communication imperatives* in Ephesians 4, especially verses 1-3, 15-16, and 25-32." Whatever else "Leading Decisively and Faithfully" means, it must be expressed in and through the grid of a **grace-filled communication filter** that values and respects people as individuals created by God and worthy to be viewed as His children. The Triune God grieves when His people relate to others no differently than non-believers relate to each other.

The following poem by the late family therapist Virginia Satir (1976) expresses the essence of what it means to speak the truth in love:

GOALS FOR ME
I want to love you without clutching,
appreciate you without judging,
join you without invading,
invite you without demanding,
leave you without guilt,
criticize you without blaming,
and help you without insulting.
If I can have the same from you,
then we can truly meet and
enrich each other. (p. 3)

Conflict situations do arise in faith communities. What a difference it makes, however, when we affirm that the person "across the table" from us with whom we are in conflict, on the basis of his/her testimony of faith, is a brother or sister in Christ, and a member, with me, of the body of Christ!

With this perspective in mind, review Ephesians 4:25-32 to identify reasons for speaking the truth in love as we live and lead.

1. We "speak the truth in love" because: "We are members of one body." (Ephesians 4:25)

In Paul's letter to the Ephesians, he has much to say to us about our conversations with others. Because of our faith conviction to speak the truth in love, we should "put off falsehood" (Ephesians 4:25). We should not lie. Paul was speaking to Christians. This verse applied particularly in areas of emotional dishonesty — not being honest with others regarding my negative feelings toward them when barriers between us have been created. John Powell (1999) explained the levels of communication on which we speak:

- Lowest level - the level of cliché
- Next level - the level of facts
- A higher level - the level of idea
- An even higher level - the level of feelings
  (pp. 50-62)

Paul encourages us to be honest. With the awareness that we are accepted comes the freedom to be honest. New Testament injunctions to "speak the truth one to another," imply far more than an absence of lies. It implies the kind of honesty that *allows others to know us as we are*, secure in our acceptance by God and by them, and based on the affirming experience of love. Satir (1976) calls this emotional honesty, "*congruence.*" She stated, "Being emotionally honest is the heart of making contact" (p. 11).

Even when under attack, the apostle Paul opened his heart to others, to share with them his inner feelings and experiences (i.e., II Corinthians 1:3-9, 2:1-4). He could claim without hesitation that the religious leaders of the day were labeled hypocrites because they were always focusing on externals as the measure of one's faith. It is probable that their lifestyles finally meant that they were deceiving themselves as well as attempting to deceive others. How striking it is that the Pharisees are the one group of people whom Jesus was unable to touch. They had lost contact with reality, lived in their own world of pretense, and were cut off from all that could have saved them.

John deals with the issue of honesty in his first epistle. In insisting that we "walk in the light," he first points us to the necessity of being honest with ourselves (and others) about our sins and failings (I John 1:1-9). Freedom to know

God's progressive cleansing comes only with honesty about our sins and confession of them. A context in the fellowship of believers is imperative where believers can be honest with one another, take on one another's burdens, where forgiveness can be requested and freely given, and confessions made.

Why is this so important? Paul refers to followers of Christ as members of one body (v. 25). Read the following passages that also describe our relationship to one another.

I Corinthians 12:12-27

[12]*The body is a unit, though it is made up of many parts; and though all its parts are many, they form one body. So it is with Christ.* [13]*For we were all baptized by one Spirit into one body--whether Jews or Greeks, slave or free--and we were all given the one Spirit to drink.* [14]*Now the body is not made up of one part but of many.* [15]*If the foot should say, "Because I am not a hand, I do not belong to the body," it would not for that reason cease to be part of the body.* [16]*And if the ear should say, "Because I am not an eye, I do not belong to the body," it would not for that reason cease to be part of the body.* [17]*If the whole body were an eye, where would the sense of hearing be? If the whole body were an ear, where would the sense of smell be?* [18]*But in fact God has arranged the parts in the body, every one of them, just as he wanted them to be.* [19]*If they were all one part, where would the body be?* [20]*As it is, there are many parts, but one body.*

[21]*The eye cannot say to the hand, "I don't need you!" And the head cannot say to the feet, "I don't need you!"* [22]*On the contrary, those parts of the body that seem to be weaker are indispensable,* [23]*and the parts that we think are less honorable we treat with special honor. And the parts that are unpresentable are treated with special modesty,*

35

[superscript]24[/superscript]*while our presentable parts need no special treatment. But God has combined the members of the body and has given greater honor to the parts that lacked it,* [superscript]25[/superscript]*so that there should be no division in the body, but that its parts should have equal concern for each other.* [superscript]26[/superscript]*If one part suffers, every part suffers with it; if one part is honored, every part rejoices with it.* [superscript]27[/superscript]*Now you are the body of Christ, and each one of you is a part of it.*

I Peter 3:8-9, 13-17

[superscript]8[/superscript]*Finally, all of you, live in harmony with one another; be sympathetic, love as brothers, be compassionate and humble.* [superscript]9[/superscript]*Do not repay evil with evil or insult with insult, but with blessing, because to this you were called so that you may inherit a blessing.*

[superscript]13[/superscript]*Who is going to harm you if you are eager to do good?* [superscript]14[/superscript]*But even if you should suffer for what is right, you are blessed. "Do not fear what they fear; do not be frightened."* [superscript]15[/superscript]*But in your hearts set apart Christ as Lord. Always be prepared to give an answer to everyone who asks you to give the reason for the hope that you have. But do this with gentleness and respect,* [superscript]16[/superscript]*keeping a clear conscience, so that those who speak maliciously against your good behavior in Christ may be ashamed of their slander.* [superscript]17[/superscript]*It is better, if it is God's will, to suffer for doing good than for doing evil.*

Romans 12:3-8

[superscript]3[/superscript]*For by the grace given me I say to every one of you: Do not think of yourself more highly than you ought, but rather think of yourself with sober judgment, in accordance with the measure of faith God has given you.* [superscript]4[/superscript]*Just as each of us has one body with many members, and these members do not all have the same function,* [superscript]5[/superscript]*so in Christ we who are many form one body, and each* member belongs to all the others. [6]We have different gifts, according to the grace given us. If a man's gift is prophesying, let him use it in proportion to his faith. [7]If it is serving, let him serve; if it is teaching, let him teach; [8]if it is encouraging, let him encourage; if it is contributing to the needs of others, let him give generously; if it is leadership, let him govern diligently; if it is showing mercy, let him do it cheerfully.

Ephesians 4:1-6

[1]As a prisoner for the Lord, then, I urge you to live a life worthy of the calling you have received. [2]Be completely humble and gentle; be patient, bearing with one another in love. [3]Make every effort to keep the unity of the Spirit through the bond of peace. [4]There is one body and one Spirit--just as you were called to one hope when you were called-- [5]one Lord, one faith, one baptism; [6]one God and Father of all, who is over all and through all and in all.

2. We "speak the truth in love" because: " Satan gets a foothold in our lives when we do not... " (Ephesians 4:26-27).

Therefore, do not delay. ("Do not let the sun go down on your anger.") You should respond in a Christian manner. ("In your anger do not sin.") The issue of conflict is real within the Christian community and must be addressed.

In conflict management, the key issue is understanding, not agreement!

The goal is not conflict resolution, but conflict management in a Christianly manner. Conflict exists in relationships in the local church, a Christian university, and the Christian home. We need to talk about it. Too often we use avoidance tactics in conflict situations.

37

Avoidance tactics in conflict management is denying the issue by not talking about the situation or by talking around or past the person instead of dealing with the given circumstances. This approach or avoidance tactic continually puts off the "real" issue until "tomorrow" or the next meeting, believing that it will eventually go away. Often, we make the un-scriptural assumption that 'peace-loving' Christians should get along and not really have serious conflicts. We all know this isn't true but still avoid the issue.

We deny our real feelings; harbor resentment, and allow the bitterness to intensify. We lack the knowledge of how to deal creatively in conflict situations. We're afraid to share our honest feelings for fear of rejection, disapproval, frustration, or hurt. We want to protect our *image* of being nice, kind, understanding, and loving.

Conflict is what develops between individuals when they differ. David Augsburger (1983), in his book, *Caring to Confront*, stated, "When your thrust as a person runs counter to mine, to deny my own thrust is to be untrue to the push and the pull of God within me. For me to ignore and do violence to your thrust as a person is to violate your becoming a Son of God" (p. 53).

Augsburger (1983) continued, "Conflict is natural, normal and neutral. Conflict is neither good nor bad, right nor wrong. Conflict simply is. And how we view, approach and work through our differences does to a large extent determine our whole life pattern" (p. 6). The question is not *will* conflict arise? The question is *how* do we deal with it?

Virginia Satir (1972) believed that "Communication is the greatest single factor affecting one's personal health and his relationship to others" (p. 58). She concluded from her research and studies that approximately 96% of

38

troubled families communicate within the home in one of four "inappropriate" (p. 58) ways:

1. Placate (give in)
   She says, "I told you not to say anything to others." He says, "You're right, I'm wrong. You are the leader."

2. Blame
   "Those other workers took you away from your office so you were not there when I needed you."

3. Withdraw
   He says, "What do you talk about when you get together for the afternoon break?" She leaves without saying anything. She says, "Why aren't you available by phone when we need you? He leaves without a response.

4. Distract
   She says, "We need to work on our finances, they are out of balance." He says, "You were out with that group again, weren't you?" (pp. 58, 78-79)

Although Satir (1972) addressed inappropriate communication patterns in *dysfunctional* families (pp. 78-79), one could also applied her findings to troubled *church "families,"* who relate to each other within the fellowship of faith in similar *dysfunctional and ineffective* ways. The parallels are painfully obvious.

In faith communities, including family units, local congregations, colleges, universities, and ministry organizations, "inappropriate" communication sometimes raises its ugly head. In these moments we, as decisive leaders who are faithful Christians, affirm that grace-enabled communication with God and others in a faith community is perhaps the greatest single factor affecting one's personal health, her and his relationship with others, and the pursuit of Christlikeness.

The result of using the four inappropriate ways is that the problem remains, tension mounts, and the relationship is edgy.

There is a fifth option. Augsburger (1983) calls it "care-fronting," or "caring enough to confront" (p. 11). Satir's (1972) description is "Leveling with integrity" (p. 72). For the Apostle Paul, it is "Speaking the truth in love" (Ephesians 4:15).

Care-fronting or "leveling" leads to the biblical principle of "speaking the truth in love." This option brings healing, enables growth, and produces change. There are two arms of a genuine relationship— confrontation with truth and affirmation of love.

So how can I begin to manage conflict in a "caring and confronting" way?

First, eliminate a win/lose mentality (I'm right, you're wrong). There are three methods of the win/lose mentality: I win, you lose; you win, I lose; no win.

Reaching out is two-sided based on others' needs and our own needs. With left hand reaching out—I do care; I want to respect you; I want your respect; and with the right hand reaching out—I want you to know how I feel; I want to tell you where I am; I have this goal for our relationship. This "caring and confronting" approach ends the blaming game and gets to healing questions—in simple, clear, direct language.

You must ask yourself: Where do we start? What is the loving, responsible, truly respectful thing to do? Where do we go from here?

Second, practice "active listening." This practice involves hearing with an inner ear to the feelings, hurts, angers, and the demands of the other person. An active listener truly hears what another person says; how it is said; and what feelings are conveyed.

Third, use "I" messages instead of "You" messages. "I" messages reflect my feelings without placing blame. "You" messages are often attacks, criticisms, faultfinding of the other person, labels, and ways of fixing blame. There is a significant difference between an honest confessional ("I" message) and distorted rejection ("You" message) (see Table 2.1).

Table 2.1. "I" and "You" Messages

"I" Message	"You" Message
I am angry.	You make me angry.
I feel rejected.	You're judging and rejecting me.
I don't like the wall between us.	You're building a wall between us.
I don't like being blamed or bearing blame.	You're blaming everything on me.
I want freedom to say yes or no.	You're trying to run my life.
I want a respectful friendship with you again.	You've got to respect me or you're not my friend.

Fourth, eliminate "why" questions. "Why" questions are an effective way of manipulating others — similar to "You" messages: "Why do you always leave your things lying all over the house? Why don't you pick up after yourselves? Why don't you show a little interest in things? Why can't I get a little cooperation?" We use "why" questions to give hidden messages of anger that we are unwilling to own honestly. "Why" questions are like a *hit and run.*

Fifth, give clear "yes" or "no" signals. "Yes" signals come easy; however, "No" signals come very hard — especially face-to-face. Often we hesitate to state our feelings clearly — for fear of rejection or disapproval of others. Jesus said, "Let your 'yes' be a clear 'yes' and your 'no,' 'no.'"

We tend to respond to wrongs done to us in an equally *wrong* way.

Sixth, initiate discussion if you have a complaint. Accept anger as a normal, natural human emotion. Clear statements of anger are something different than feelings and demands. Clear statements are a positive emotion, a self-affirming emotion that responds to the heart of rejection and devastation. There are two types of anger to consider — personal anger and virtuous anger, which is anger focused on deed not person. Virtuous anger can slice through emotional barriers or communication barriers and establish contacts.

"Speaking the truth in love," "caring enough to confront," and "truthing" it with integrity are the Christ-like responses to conflict.

These responses describe a lifestyle for Christians who care enough to confront where conflicts arise. Read again Ephesians 4:15-32. When differences between people are dealt with openly, conflict can be a positive experience because it can lead to personal growth. However, when differences are concealed and individuals are prevented from expressing themselves, personal growth will not occur.

Personal conflict is a part of growing up and trying out new capabilities. Learn the value of expressing differences openly and kindly. Listen to the other person's response. Seek understanding.

Positive questions (see Figure 2.2) to ask in the midst of conflict situations are: What can *I* learn? How can *I* change? These are *growth-producing* questions. On the contrary, *growth-inhibiting* questions are: Why me? What if…? This is the *could have, should have, would have* way of thinking.

Growth - Producing Questions:
What can I learn? How can I change?

Growth - Inhibiting Questions:
Why me? What if…?

Figure 2.2. Two ways of thinking and reacting to conflict. © E.L. Fairbanks

**3. We "speak the truth in love" because: "
The power of words can heal and affirm"
(Ephesians 4:29).**

"*Speak only what is helpful for building others up according to their needs*" (Ephesians 4:29). Paul encourages members of the Body to use their speech for the help of others, for their up-building as the occasion may offer.

Our speech is to be used for the benefit of those who are linked with us in the body of Christ. *Dialogue is a sacrament.* We are to converse with each other within the fellowship in such a way that our words become a vehicle and demonstration of the very grace of God. In all conversation, the choice of language and subject matter has to be such that the affirmation and edification are for the purpose of "ministering grace" to the hearer. For Paul, there is no room for empty chatter or for remarks that serve no other purpose than to degrade another person.

Colossians 4:6 reads, "*Let your conversation be always full of grace, seasoned with salt, so that you may know how to answer everyone.*" In biblical anthropology, the mouth is representative of the whole body and reveals the whole man. In Matthew 12:34, Jesus said, "*Out of the overflow of the heart, the mouth speaks.*"

Saint Paul emphasized that one's speech reveals the quality of his relationship with Christ. Paul is not talking about a *technique* but an *attitude of the heart toward* the other person. I *need* you—you have gifts and strengths I don't have. I *love* you—You are my brother/sister in Christ. I *accept* you—Christ is changing you, as I am being changed. I *trust* you—you desire to serve the same Christ I serve. I *respect* you—you are different; yet, we are one in Christ. I *serve* you—I want to *minister grace* to you.

In his book, *The Way of the Heart: Desert Spirituality and Contemporary Spirituality*, Nouwen (1991) stated, "When the door of the steam bath is continually left open, the heat inside escapes through it" (p. 52). How often we

44

open our mouths and speak about events of the world, about people, or circumstances, and how seldom we close our mouths to listen to God and to others? Psalms 39:1 reminds us, "I will keep a muzzle on my mouth...I will not...let my tongue lead me into sin."

It is a matter of the focus of our words – "*only what is helpful for building others up, according to their needs, that it may benefit those who listen*" (Ephesians 4:29b). There must be a focus beyond ourselves, beyond self-serving comments. Our focus must be on the building up of others. Clinical psychologist, Sven Wahlroos (1974), in his book, *Family Communication*, stated, "Make your communication as realistically positive as possible" (p. 25). As a guideline, he said, "The praise to criticism ratio should be kept at about 90-80 percent praise to 10-20 percent criticism" (pp. 28-29).

Usually the opposite is true in our interactions with others. Sometimes being emotionally honest necessitates criticism of another in an appropriate manner. However, 80-90% praise is needed (i.e., Thank you, I appreciate you; you were helpful; you affirmed me, I am grateful for you). It cannot be superficial, or it will be resented.

The words we use in leading decisively raise some very personal and practical questions to consider as we measure our words.

Consider these questions regarding the use of our words within the community of faith?

1. Does what I say build up or tear down the other person?

2. Would I say what I am saying directly to the person involved?

45

3. Do I know all the facts, or am I responding on the basis of half-truths or partial facts?

4. Is my response triggered more by emotion than by reason?

5. Is the issue really deserving of the action and energy that I am giving it?

6. Can the situation be seen from a different perspective?

7. Have I tried to accept the feelings of the other person and understand why the person feels the ways/he does?

> IF IT DOESN'T MAKE A DIFFERENCE
> DON'T LET IT MAKE A DIFFERENCE.

Ephesians 4:28a tells us to steal no longer. The broader implications of this passage prohibits the sin of slander, tale-bearing, gossip, flattery, and "character assassination" as in Exodus 20:16, *"Ye shall not bear false witness against your neighbor."* To destroy a man's character by a whispering campaign profits nothing. As Shakespeare put it: "Who steals my purse steals trash; ...But he that filches from me my good name; Robs me of that which not enriches him, and makes me poor indeed."– Othello, Act III, Scene 3, Line 183.

We have the power to bless. All who have influence have the power to bless and to withhold blessings, to cause others to grow or to wither, to help or to hinder, to heal or to hurt. The person who can *speak* the sincere word of forgiveness and acceptance is a *healer* of the highest order.

> Paul is concerned with the role of words exchanged
> between individuals within the body.
> In the midst of everyday dialog, God's *grace and
> power* should flow through the words we use.

**4. We "speak the truth in love" because:
"We have been forgiven in Christ" (Ephesians 4:31-32).**

The command is clear, we are to be forgiving just as
Christ forgave us. Ephesians 4:32 implies that through
love, the barriers to fellowship can be set aside.

An attitude of "realized forgiveness" describes the
climate in the faith community. But what if it is not? You
must take initiative in forgiving *regardless* of the response
of the other person. Realized forgiveness creates a growing
desire to build up the other in love. A climate in which
persons are so close to one another and so confident of
acceptance that sharing burdens, forgiving, even taking the
other to task is no threat to the relationship. There must be
no room for strife, resentment, or envy (Ephesians 4:31).
God's forgiveness enables the Christian to find his way
back to the one from whom he is alienated. You must
forgive *others*, for God in Christ has forgiven *you*.

The issue is not so much the response from others to
our efforts to be kind, compassionate, and forgiving. Our
efforts may not always be received in the spirit they
were given. Withholding forgiveness creates bitterness;
anger increases; resentment manifests itself; and Satan
laughs.

Our calling is to be Christ-like even in the
uncomfortable situations in which we sometimes find
ourselves. God will provide blessing and joy *within* us,
regardless of the apparent rejection of others. Remember,

as believers, we forgive—not to change people—but because God, in Christ, forgave us. And we were so undeserving. Sometimes, we have been hurt so deeply that we cannot reach out with integrity, in forgiveness to others. "Father...forgive them...." The words of Jesus were words of a **prayer!**

Paul reminds us that God's *Grace* is sufficient for us in our weakness, and His *power* is made perfect in our weakness (II Corinthians 12:9).

I remember receiving numerous emails from the campus community where I served as president for 18 years. Accusations were made at me and other university personnel. The words hurt. I had a choice. I could "brew" over the stinging emails, or I could genuinely seek forgiveness, asking God to teach me through the painful situations.

God is grieved (Ephesians 4:30a). Ephesians 4:25-32 describes a lifestyle by which believers are to live together as the People of God and to lead decisively and faithfully. What happens when they don't? God is *grieved* (Ephesians 4:30a).

Does the reference in Ephesians 4:30 regarding "grieving God" refer to verse 29 or 31? The answer is both. The Spirit of God is greatly concerned about the speech of His people. The words we speak as we communicate with others are profoundly *theological* in nature. Anything that tends to destroy fellowship grieves the Spirit who seeks to build it up. The sin of offending a brother by a false word or act especially grieves God. The Spirit either rejoices or grieves with the words expressed in the fellowship.

Ephesians 4 and 5 speak directly to this issue. Read again Ephesians 4:1-3, 11, 15-16, 25 and then 5:1-2, 18-21. We are to be *"imitators* of God...and live a life of *love"* (5:1-

2) in leading others and living together as the People of God. We are to model a Christ-like lifestyle (5:1-2) and lead decisively with a vision to serve within this *theological* and *biblical* context. When we do not live like this, we grieve the Holy Spirit. **Relationships within a faith community are an intensely theological issue.** The power for this lifestyle can only be maintained, developed, and strengthened as we are continuously being filled with the Spirit (5:18). The Spirit of Christ within us empowers us to live and lead as servant leaders!

Is this communication lifestyle possible simply by *human* efforts alone? Obviously not. In Chapter 5 verse 18, Paul challenges the People of God with an imperative, "Be filled with God's Spirit...continually, daily...." The Spirit energizes the believer and provides the *power* to speak Christ-like words to those living under the sovereignty of the Spirit. As we live, lead, and relate to one another in the power of the Spirit, with a passion for the mind of Christ, the faith community is gradually transformed into the image of Christ (II Corinthians 3:18).

Intentionally Nurturing the Christ-like Life

How do we *intentionally* nurture the spiritual life within us and within others for mission and ministry effectiveness in the midst of our family, our work, and our many other commitments?

In Exodus, Chapters 3 and 4, God instructs Moses to lead his people out of Egypt. When Moses hesitates and asks God to send someone else, God underscores the concept of A in Figure 2.3. Not only did God reassure Moses, saying that He would be with Moses, but He also told Moses, *"It is I – the great 'I am' - who calls, empowers, keeps and carries you"* (Exodus 3:14). First and foremost,

God reassured Moses of A; and He reassured Moses that armed with A, Moses would have God's power and guidance for B, to live, speak, and lead with the "mind of Christ."

Using the late Henri Nouwen's (1989) work, we will look at A, then relate A with its implications for B. Nouwen's work underscored the iterative aspect of A, showing that we play a role in activating the power God offers us. As leaders, dealing with A and B becomes a collaborative and trust-filled relationship.

Figure 2.3. The power for leading decisively. © E.L. Fairbanks

Although the Power involved in leading the people of God may appear to reside mostly in area B, in fact, the Power comes from Christ as shown in A; and this power from Christ is something we as leaders are continually receiving, reflecting, and pursuing, hence the circular diagram. Your leadership style is a reflection of how you respond to the power (B) Christ offers you. Most of this chapter explores area B; however, it is essential to take a moment to explore the source of the leader's strength to speak to, not past, each other.

In discussing the subject of "Christian Leadership," Henri Nouwen clearly recognized that both **A** and **B** in Figure 2.3 are to be considered when looking at the speech and conduct of Christian leaders. In the discussion of Nouwen's book and the Bible study of Philippians 2, we will focus primarily on A in Figure 2.3.

In the Name of Jesus: Reflections on Christian Leadership captures an address by Henri Nouwen in 1989 to a group of Roman Catholic leaders in Washington, D.C. Nouwen had several years earlier moved to Daybreak, one of the L'Arche communities worldwide for mentally handicapped people. Nouwen's move to Daybreak in Toronto, Canada, followed his brilliant teaching career at Harvard, Yale, and Notre Dame.

The brief, yet powerful, book of 81 pages focused on a vision of Christian leadership nurtured in a life of prayer, confession, and forgiveness in community. Nouwen (1989) deftly addressed three contemporary temptations of Christian leaders — to be **relevant**, to be **spectacular**, and to be **powerful** — and is guided in his vision by two stories from the Gospels: the story of Jesus' temptation in the desert (Matthew 4:1-11) and the story of Peter's call to be a shepherd (John 21:15-19).

Christian leadership, according to Nouwen (1989), involved self-denial and leads from vulnerability to God's power. As is often the case with Nouwen (1989), he identified three "movements" in the book:

- From Relevance to Prayer
- From Popularity to Ministry
- From Leading to being Led (pp. 13-65)

Nouwen (1989) reminded us that Jesus' first temptation was to be relevant: to turn stones to bread. To this temptation, Nouwen's words are clear:

The leader of the future will be the one who dares to claim his irrelevance in the contemporary world as a divine vocation that allows him or her to enter into a deep solidarity with the anguish underlying all the glitter of success and to bring the light of Jesus there. (p. 22)

The "irrelevance" is rooted in the permanent, intimate relationship with the incarnate Word, Jesus, and for leaders to find there the source for their words, advice, and guidance. Nouwen's "irrelevance" is the subject of **A** in Figure 2.3.

Remember the second temptation of Jesus? It was a temptation to do something spectacular, something that would bring the applause of people, something that would highlight **B** in Figure 2.3. "Throw yourself from the parapet of the temple and let the angels catch you and carry you in their arms," the enemy told Jesus. The discipline needed to counter this temptation to be popular and do something spectacular is the discipline of confession and forgiveness. Nouwen (1989) reminded us that in our strength we cannot heal, reconcile, or give life to others. We are "wounded" people who need as much care as those we serve. "The mystery of ministry," Nouwen proclaimed, "is that we have been chosen to make our own limited and very conditional love the gateway for the unlimited and unconditional love of God" (p. 44).

The discipline required to overcome the temptation of "individual heroism" (or look to **A** instead of **B**) is confession and forgiveness—individuals willing to confess their brokenness and to ask forgiveness from those to whom they minister. Making humble connections (confession and forgiveness) to those we lead helps the Christian leader overcome the temptation of "individual heroism." Christian leaders "are called to live the Incarnation, that is, to live in their own bodies but also in the corporate body of the community, and to discover there the presence of the Holy Spirit" (Nouwen, 1989, p. 48). In the faith communities, we are "accountable to them, and need their affection and support, and are called to minister with their whole being, including their wounded selves" (p. 50).

The third temptation of Jesus was the temptation of power. "I will give you all the Kingdoms of this world in their splendor," Jesus was told by Satan (again, a **B** focus in Figure 2.3). Is this an irresistible temptation? Nouwen (1989) reminded us that power provides a substitute for "the hard task of love, control over the cross, being a leader over being led" (p. 60). Power, control, and being a leader are often substituted, Nouwen believed, for healthy, intimate relationships with the faith community.

John 21:18, especially the words, "Somebody else will take you where you would rather not go," is a pivotal passage for Christian leaders, according to Nouwen (1989), who desired to let go of personal power and to follow the humble way of Jesus. The ability and willingness to be *led where you would rather not go* is crucial.

Nouwen (1989) challenged Christian leaders to think theologically about the practice of leadership—thinking and leading with the mind of Christ. Christian leaders think, speak, and act in the name of Jesus.

The Christian leaders of the future have to be theologians, persons who know the heart of God and are trained—through prayer, study, and careful analysis—to manifest the divine event of God's saving work in the midst of the many seemingly random events of their time (p. 68).

In referring to leading with the mind of Christ, Nouwen (1989) presented a *theological* leadership—a deep spiritual formation involving the whole person: body, mind, and spirit. Nouwen asked us to move from a leadership built on personal power to a leadership in which we critically discern where God is leading us and the people we lead. (p. 72). This requires us to be **A**-focused. Are we willing to be led "where we do not want to go" (John 21:18)

In the book, *Daring Greatly*, Brene Brown (2012) speaks powerfully about the courage needed to be vulnerable, and how this vulnerability transforms the way we live and lead. Rather than sitting on the sidelines, keeping quiet, and harboring resentment, she encourages us to "show up," to be all in and let ourselves be seen and heard. She refers to this as vulnerability, and from her perspective, it is "daring greatly." It is "speaking the truth in love" without knowing how the other person(s) will receive your words or respond to them.

During a 1999 research sabbatical at the Yale University Divinity School in which I had access to the complete works of Henri Nouwen, including his course lectures, journal articles, and books, it became increasingly apparent that focusing on the Triune God was a necessary marker to successful personal change and external impact. I needed to reinvigorate my pursuit for Christlikeness.

Throughout the reading of *this* book, I encourage you to keep a journal to capture insights gained from your study of each "marker," as outlined in the Introduction of the book. Pay particular attention to scriptural passages that become "foundation stones" as you seek to lead the People of God decisively and faithfully. Begin with some passages that are pivotal for you in your calling to lead others in a faith community, passage such as:

"But seek first his kingdom and his righteousness, and all these things will be given to you." Matthew 6:33

"We teach spiritual things spiritually." I Corinthians 2:13

"But we have the mind of Christ." I Corinthians 2:16b

"But we have this treasure in jars of clay to show that this all surpassing power is from God and not from us."
II Corinthians 4:7

"So from now on we regard no one from a worldly point of view." II Corinthians 5:16a

"Instead, speaking the truth in love, we will in all things grow up into him who is the Head, that is Christ." Ephesians 4:15

"Do not let any unwholesome talk come out of your mouths, but only what is helpful for building others up according to their needs, that it may benefit those who listen." Ephesians 4:29

We have now explored the relationship between the PASSION for and the IMPERATIVE in leading decisively within the communities we serve. The power of servant leaders is rooted in the pursuit to relate to others with "the mind of Christ" (I Corinthians 2:16b).

The pursuit of Christlikeness enables us to "speak the truth in love" more clearly and consistently with the "mind of Christ" within us, as we communicate with one another within faith communities. We now turn our attention to the goal of the ministry to which we are all called and to those who join us in ministry as the Body of Christ, the People of God, and the Fellowship of the Spirit.

MAKING CONTACT
Virginia Satir (1976)

I believe the greatest gift
I can conceive of having from anyone is
to be seen by them,
heard by them,
to be understood
and touched by them.
The greatest gift
I can give is
to see, hear, understand,
and to touch another person.
When this is done
I feel contact has been made. (p. 1)

MARKER THREE:

THE GOAL OF LEADING DECISIVELY IS FOCUSED ON EFFECTIVELY PREPARING THE BODY OF CHRIST– THE PEOPLE OF GOD–FOR MINISTRY AND MISSION.

Chapter Three

MARKER THREE:
THE GOAL OF LEADING DECISIVELY IS FOCUSED ON EFFECTIVELY PREPARING THE BODY OF CHRIST — THE PEOPLE OF GOD — FOR MINISTRY AND MISSION.

The Christian ministry is a shared ministry with every believer serving and supporting one another, using Holy Spirit-given gifts to stimulate personal and corporate growth and reconciliation in both the church and the world.

Edward LeBron Fairbanks

The purpose of servant leading is to *shape* Christ-like disciples and leaders in the local congregation, college or university, or ministry organization. This vision is our passion for the people of God we serve, as discussed in Marker One. *How* we lead, teach, and preach to help others realize their calling for Christ is both the challenge and the focus of this chapter.

Modeling, or setting the example, was at the very core of first-century teaching about discipleship: *"And the things you have heard me say in the presence of many witnesses entrust to reliable people who will also be qualified to teach others"* (II Timothy 2:2).

Just after its publication in 1977, I read the book *Servant Leadership*, by Robert Greenleaf, former Director of Management Research for AT&T. I had recently started my first administrative and teaching assignment in Christian higher education. Greenleaf's book had a tremendous impact on me.

The second chapter of *Servant Leadership* (1977) focused on "The Institution as Servant." Greenleaf (2002) stated:

> ...caring for persons, the more able and the less able serving each other, is the rock upon which a good society is built. Whereas, until recently, caring was largely person-to-person, now most of it is mediated through institutions–often large, complex, powerful, impersonal, not always competent, sometimes corrupt. If a better society is to be built, one that is more just and more loving, one that provides greater creative opportunity for its people, then the most open course is to *raise both the capacity to serve* and the *very performance as servant* of existing major institutions by the generative forces operating within them. (p. 96)

If believers in Jesus the Christ are committed to a lifestyle of ministry and mission, then nonprofit and ministry organizations, colleges and universities, and local congregations must, to use Greenleaf's (1977) words, "raise both the capacity to serve and the very performance of a servant" (p. 96). This improvement will only happen as organization leaders, pastors, board members, teachers, sector leaders, volunteers, and a host of others in the community of faith *model a servant lifestyle.*

How do we as members of a local church or ministry organization exemplify a lifestyle transformation for both those we lead and those who lead us? How do we teach the necessity for change in values, priorities, commitments, character qualities, and an understanding that transformation is a lifelong pursuit? How do we communicate with each other so that the Christian faith is presented not as an intellectualized belief to be learned, but a life to be lived? How can we live together in a community of faith so that, to use Greenleaf's (1977) words, "caring for persons, the more able and the less able serving each other" (p. 96) increasingly characterizes the members of the faith community and the local church as a caring institution?

Ephesians 4:11-16 enunciates such a model. The passage outlines the context, task, goal, dynamic, and purpose for us as Christian leaders in our passion to equip the people we lead for a lifestyle of service.

The context...is "God's people" (Ephesians 4:11-12). The key focus is participation.

Since all Christians are called to serve others in Jesus' name, all Christians are also called to prepare others in this lifestyle of service. Learning is not limited to the students in the classroom. It permeates all the different roles and responsibilities to which we commit ourselves. All of us are on a spiritual pilgrimage and are in process of becoming what God the Father, Creator, and Redeemer envisions for us.

The task...is to "prepare God's people" (Ephesians 4:12). The key idea is formation.

Christian formation, or preparing God's people, means enabling the individual to grow in Christ-likeness. This demands an acquaintance with the Christian tradition, awareness of community, understanding of national and world issues, on-going development of personal faith, a knowledge of key scriptures, an increase in competence in vocational skills, a maturing philosophy of life, a global perspective, and growth in community.

"Spiritual formation is the process of being conformed to the image of Christ for the sake of others"

(Mulholland, 1993, p.15). We need guidance in developing a lifestyle of devotion to Christ, in caring for the world, nurturing our own spiritual lives, relating to other world citizens, developing personal qualities, and inculcating values by which we live and die.

The goal...is "works of service" (Ephesians 4:12). The key thought is expression.

Our "works of service" or mission is a function and expression of the People of God. Our goal is to prepare God's people to participate in this mission, to proclaim the kingdom of God, to nurture the People of God, and to serve the whole human community. We must be captured by this vision. In a university setting, this means transcending service *to* the students and *for* the students, to service *with* the students and *by* the students. The same can be said for ministry organizations, community nonprofits, and those who identify the local faith community as their church home.

The dynamic...is "love within the Body of Christ" (Ephesians 4:15-16). The key concept is interaction.

Interaction is defined as an intimacy of relationship between members within the Body of Christ. In every New Testament passage where the Body of Christ is discussed, there is a relational context in which this kind of mutual nurturing takes place. Passing on information does not produce a servant of Christ. Trust needs both to be explained and demonstrated in an intimate relationship context. Love and trust free us to know and reveal ourselves to one another. Modeling, rather than indoctrinating, is the method of leadership for lifestyle change.

The purpose...is transformation for a "holiness lifestyle" (Ephesians 4:13). The key issue is Christ-likeness.

The purpose of Christian leadership is to, by grace, *participate with God in the reconciling and transforming of humankind,* so that holy people may be equipped for a Christ-like ministry of service to others as they fulfill their vocational responsibility. A holiness lifestyle focuses on the progressive transformation of the Christian toward the character, values, motives, attitudes, and understanding of God Himself.

The Primary Method of Teaching for Transformation

The primary method of teaching for transformation, I believe, is modeling or "exampling." Our challenge is to *intentionally* nurture those whom we lead for mission and ministry accomplishment in the midst of *their* family, *their* work, and *their* many other commitments.

In other words, how do we determine if we have succeeded in our teaching and leadership assignment to prepare *others* for *their* ministry and mission? What definition of success did Jesus use?

In general terms, we begin to answer the questions when we understand ourselves as servants — motivating, equipping, and enabling others to serve in Jesus' name. We want those for whom we are responsible to see in us a *servant spirit* committed to motivating, equipping, and enabling them to serve *others* in Jesus' name. The *ministry* of equipping others to serve others in the name of Jesus (Ephesians 4:12b-13) is paramount for the leader.

Equipping those for whom we are responsible (Ephesians 4:12) means that we prepare others to reproduce themselves in the work to which they are called (see also II Timothy 2:2). We equip them in such a way that the *students* will be like their teachers, pastors, professors, or mentors. The crucial concern is for every believer to participate in the ministry of reconciliation as God has gifted, called, and "stationed" her or him.

As a leader, how do you teach this *lifestyle*? You teach a servant lifestyle through the principle of *imitation*. Luke 6:40 challenges us: "*...When a student is fully trained he will become like his teacher.*" Modeling the message suggests that teachers and leaders create a learning environment that exhibits in practice what is said in word. "Exampling" implies an emotional closeness between the leader and the led within the body of Christ. Reflect on Paul's admonitions:

- *"Follow me as I follow Christ"* (I Corinthians. 11:1).
- *"You ought to follow my example"* (II Thessalonians 3:7).
- *"Put into practice what you have learned, received or heard from me or seen in me..."* (Philippians 4:9).
- *"We did this in order to make ourselves a model for you to follow"* (II Thessalonians 3:9).

He gave gifts...to some... to guide and teach his people... so that Christians might be properly equipped for their service.... That the body might be built up...until we arrive at real maturity.... (Therefore) we are meant to speak the truth in love, and to grow up in every way unto Christ, the head (Ephesians 4:11-16).

The Ephesians passage helps us in answering our primary concern: How can we teach and lead so that the Christian faith is experienced not as "intellectual belief" to be known but as a *life* to be lived and shared? We can teach others to *know*, but how do we teach them to live a Christian lifestyle and to lead Christianly? The answers to these and other related questions come when we more clearly understand our task to be "the equipping of believers"; the goal of our work to be "service or ministry through believers"; and the method to be "modeling or an emotional closeness between the leader and the led within the body of Christ."

First Things First

Before proceeding with equipping issues, let's pause, review, and discuss God's supreme "goal" or purpose for His children. We need to get this right in our own lives and in the lives of the people we serve before we focus on preparing others for ministry and mission.

God's vision for *us* is that we be men and women of good and godly character. *"What kind of people ought you to be?"* Peter asks in his New Testament epistle. He immediately responds, *"You ought to live holy and godly lives"* (II Peter 3:11-12 NIV).

"If I take care of my character, my reputation will take care of itself." D.L. Moody
(www.goodreads.com/author/quotes/5083573.D_L_Moody)

Character is different from reputation. Reputation is what you are supposed to be; character is what you are.

Character does count. Character is what you are when nobody else is around. Character is who we are in the pressure times of our lives. Character springs from the core values by which we build our lives. Your reputation is made in a moment; your character is built in a lifetime.

Christian character provides the moral compass by which we live our lives and lead a faith community in ministry and mission.

Character captures what we most want our children to inherit from us and is the wellspring and foundation of our outward actions. Consequently, Christian character *qualities* must be intensely pursued.

I often ponder this question: Do people see in us the character qualities identified in II Peter 1:5-7? The apostle mentions the qualities of faith, goodness, knowledge (or discernment), self-control, perseverance, godliness, brotherly kindness, and love. I'm afraid people may see or hear just the opposite, like a cynical tongue, a judgmental spirit, a negative attitude, a condescending demeanor, manipulation, lying, cheating, or immorality.

If we do not guard our thoughts and spirit, these negative attitudes and behaviors, will eat us alive. Perhaps we on a college campus, a ministry organization, or in a local church have not escaped the temptation to cynicism, negativism, and condescension.

The Bible identifies different character qualities to be intensely pursued, if we are to become men and women of good and godly character...who "live holy and godly lives" (II Peter 3:11-12). Paul's list in Ephesians 4:2 includes humility, gentleness, patience, and kindness. The Old Testament prophet Micah asked, "And what does the Lord require of you but to do justly, to love mercy, and to walk humbly with your God?" Leadership is about your character—Who you are—and not your position, or what you do.

Character has powerful implications for Christian leaders. Namely, as leaders, we have a responsibility to be role models, to help build character. If what I "do" in ministry and mission does not flow from who I "am" in Christ, then a huge disconnect will be felt in the lives of those I seek to lead. Our responsibility is to model that spirit for our colleagues. This is to occur throughout the process of shaping decisive leaders who deserve to serve.

Modeling is the primary process by which leaders "pass on" the fundamental character qualities and values needed in future leaders. These qualities in our lives as leaders, or lack of them, will either confirm or deny to others what it is we want to teach them about ministry and mission.

God's vision for *us* is that we be men and women of good and godly character... individuals who live holy and godly lives.

II Peter 1:3, states, *"God's divine power has given us all things that pertain to life and godliness."* On the other hand, in verse 5, we are challenged to *"make every effort to add to your faith these qualities."* In other words, the character qualities identified by Peter flow from a life that has been saved by God's grace alone, through faith in Jesus Christ, who calls us to a life of holy living.

Yet, these very qualities of the holy life must be *nurtured, cultivated, and developed* throughout our lives and in the lives of those we lead, if we truly are to be Christlike. Christian character formation takes place over a lifetime and is shaped through our responses to scriptural imperatives, teaching, and through a process of brokenness and prayer.

I have discovered a painful yet fascinating relationship between brokenness and character development. In the conflict situations of life, I must continually ask the question: What is God needing to teach me about *my* character through *this* circumstance or through this encounter... at home, on the job, or in the church?

66

Remember the chorus set to music based on Paul's words in II Corinthians 12:9?

His strength is perfect when our strength is gone,
He will carry us when we can't carry on;
Raised in His power, the weak become strong;
His strength is perfect; His strength is perfect.

Seven questions have helped me in a lifelong pursuit of Christian character development. Perhaps, they will help you as you equip those for whom you are responsible.

1. Will this action strengthen me spiritually?

2. Would I want my child, my spouse, or my best friend to copy this action of mine?

3. Does this action violate a biblical principle?

4. Does this action strengthen the body of Christ?

5. Would an unbelieving friend be attracted to Christ and the Christian faith by my behavior?

6. Do my negative attitudes affect other people?

7. If this happens, what will I do to change this type of behavior in my life?

Maxwell and Dorman (1997), in *Becoming a Person of Influence,* stated, "many succeed momentarily by what they know, some succeed temporarily by what they do, but few succeed permanently by who they are" (p. 40)

Christian character formation is a life-changing and lifelong process, nurtured primarily by the spiritual disciplines of confession, silence, prayer, the trials and testing of our faith and made effective in our lives by His grace and His strength alone!

Godly character development begins with the transforming work of God in our lives through the new birth. Nicodemus, in John 3: 1-8, basically asked Jesus, "How do I begin this quest for a 'good and godly' character — a holy and godly life?"

Nicodemus had an excellent reputation. He belonged to the strictest religious group of the day. He observed the law. He fasted regularly and prayed often. He paid a tithe of his income and was a member of the Sanhedrin. He was one of the 70 elders who governed the religious and social life of the people. He had authority and prestige and was educated and respected in the community.

Jesus said to this man, *"You must be born again"* (John 3:3). When a person is "born again," s/he is born anew by the Spirit of God. We come alive to spiritual truth. We receive a new nature. As a child of God, we partake of the holiness of God. There is in us a radical change of conduct and character.

II Corinthians 5:17 says, *"If anyone is in Christ, he is a new creation, the old things have passed away, the new has come."* This is more than just patchwork or outward reformation. This is an inner, moral transformation.

Nicodemus was puzzled (John 3:9-12; 16-21). The new birth, or new life in Christ, is a mystery because it is a miracle of God. "God was in Christ, reconciling the world to himself" (II Corinthians 5:16-21). Christ took our sin upon himself and died in our place. He took the initiative and did for us what we could not do for ourselves.

68

So the question becomes: How will we respond to what God has done for us? We can respond in radical faith or we can remain in disbelief.

Are we living on our reputation, or do we know that we have been born again by the Spirit of God? Has Christ's character been formed in us, and are we growing and maturing in Christ-likeness? If not, I encourage you to confess that we want His life — His character — to be shaped in us. Remember, first things first.

Ponder this question:
When we complete our present ministry assignment,
will we be remembered more for our character
than for our reputation?

Peter comes down squarely on the side of godly character and holy living. Why? So that we will be effective and productive in ministry, mission living, and leading that counts for eternity.

It was important to me in the first several years at MVNU to forge a mission and vision statement that addressed twin concerns of mine — personal (including family) and professional (MVNU responsibility).

My mission and vision is to be a Christian role model and leader to my family first, and subsequently to the Mount Vernon Nazarene University community in the context of servant and visionary leadership.

I will give attention to the financial needs of my family, including retirement, and keep myself physically and emotionally conditioned to enable me to function with maximum effectiveness. I am a growing professional who gives priority time to strategic planning for the institution I serve.

In this context, I will enable and energize my family, friends, and colleagues to give their best to their unique roles and assignments. All of my activities initiate from and operate out of a pastoral calling as one who views himself first and foremost as a follower of Jesus who articulates, models, and is committed to His life and teachings.

As I approached my retirement years from full time, active, vocational ministry, I revised my mission and vision statement to read:

I want my 'senior' years to be characterized by maturing faith, nurturing family, personal growth, professional development, mentoring leaders, cultivating friendships, compassion for the poor, and passing to a new generation of Christians, particularly through writing, what has so freely been passed on to me.

On a sheet of paper with a line drawn through the middle of the paper indicating your life, designate the "flow" of your life — the highs and lows--reflecting the "timeline" of your life. Share with others the peaks above the line — when they occurred and why, as well as the lows.

If time permits, parallel this exercise for the church or group for which you now serve as leader. The highs? The lows? Why?

_____

_____

What lessons emerge regarding reconciliation and transformation, hope and character, ministry and mission? Keep first things first.

_____

_____

The Leader as Catalyst in Transforming a Community of Faith

LEADERSHIP FUNCTIONS	THEOLOGICAL PERSPECTIVES	KEY QUESTIONS	SPECIFIC TASKS	ORGANIZATIONAL CONCERNS
THE LEADER AS CATALYST IN TRANSFORMING A COMMUNITY OF FAITH				
DREAMING AND PLANNING	The People of God The Community of Faith The Body of Christ The Fellowship of the Spirit	Who are we? Where are we now? Where are we going? Why?	Clarify vision and mission Assess congregation Determine program Establish goals	Purpose
ORGANIZING AND ADMINISTERING	A Spirit-led and gifted people	How will we get there? When will we get those?	Organization and Implementation	Structure
MOTIVATING AND INSPIRING	A Ministering People Called, Gifted, Trained, Sent	Who will be responsible?	Mobilization and Energizing	Personnel
EVALUATING AND ENCOURAGING	A Growing People	Were we successful? What needs improvement? Where? When? How?	Review Feedback Encouragement Change	Organization Dynamics & Processes

Shaping a Reconciling and Transforming Ministry Through

Reaching Up	↑	Worship / Devotion
Reaching Out	→	Witness / Service / Evangelism
Reaching In	←	Christian Nurture / Spiritual Formation
Reaching Around	↻	Fellowship Community / The People of God

Figure 3.1. The leader as catalyst in transforming a community of faith. © E.L. Fairbanks

Many of the concepts discussed so far in the book are spiritual disciplines or lessons that the Holy Spirit has to teach us. The functions of a spiritual leader (Figure 3.1) serve as a catalyst in facilitating congregational transformation for ministry and mission. The leadership functions, (a) Dreaming and Planning; (b) Organizing and Administrating; (c) Motivating and Inspiring; and (d) Evaluating and Encouraging, are skills that all of us can learn and then strengthen. Most of us are not equally strong in each of the four functions. We need to listen to those around us who are different from us but who may have necessary leadership strengths and gifts that we do not possess.

As spiritual leaders, our first priority is to look to God in worship and devotion and seek God's wisdom and His guidance. After prayerfully seeking Him in prayer and in His Word, we take time to dream and plan.

The *specific tasks* of planning include clarifying our ministry and mission, *assessing* needs, determining programs, and establishing goals. Here are some *key questions* to ask:

- Who are we?
- Where are we now?
- Where are we going?
- Why?

Dreams often are the prerequisites to vision. Dream big, God-inspired dreams. We must do the things we think we cannot do. Happy are those who dream big dreams, and are willing to pay the price to see them come true.

Having a clear vision and clarifying our mission will help us set appropriate goals. It will also help us explain the *purpose* to those with whom we will be working. From a *theological* perspective, we "envision" those with whom we work and plan as the People of God, the Community of Faith, the Body of Christ, the Fellowship of the Spirit, a Spirit-led and Spirit-filled People, a Ministering People — called, gifted, trained, and sent — and a Growing People.

Once the vision is clear and your mission set, it is important to organize the process. The task is to implement the vision. Questions to ask are: "How will we get there?"

72

and "When will we get there?" Put deadline on each part of the process. You will have a much higher probability of completing your goal, if there is a date attached with it. Organizing the goals and determining when they are to be completed will give you a map or a structure to the process. It will keep you and your congregation on track.

One leadership responsibility that is often overlooked is being a good motivator. The task is to mobilize our congregation to complete the agreed-upon goals. Determine who will be responsible for each part of the process or plan. Motivation is more than generating enthusiasm and buy-in from the people being served. It is giving them the training or the tools to work on the mission. Motivating others is critical. The work that God has for us is too big to be done alone. We must help others recognize their calling and their gifts as well as train them.

Another leadership requirement is being an effective evaluator. This involves reviewing the process; acquiring feedback; and even changing the process, structure, or deadline, if changes need to be made to complete the goals. The motivating force is optimism. By assessing where we are and how we are doing, we can celebrate our successes as we reach intermediate goals. Evaluating also gives a comparison baseline as you initiate other programs, processes, and benchmarks

Equipping Others for Lifelong Discipleship Training

What is discipleship, and how is discipleship related to the mission and ministry of every follower of Christ? Dr. Dean Blevins co-authored the book, *Discovering Discipleship* (2010), an outstanding resource on discipleship and the dynamics of Christian education.

Blevins (2015) believes that "discipleship" defines our daily walk with Jesus Christ anchored in God's grace, with Christ as our guide, and the Holy Spirit our support. He describes discipleship as our journey both as individuals and as communities of faith. Discipleship "forms us into Christlikeness, challenges us to discern God's will in the church and for the world, and calls us to missional engagement in the world" (p. 8). This "shaping-seeking-serving process calls us to obedience, understanding, and dedication to the kingdom of God embodied in the teaching and ministry of Jesus" (pp. 8-9).

At its root, discipleship training is helping people grow in spiritual maturity to become more like Christ (II Corinthians 3:18). If, as decisive and faithful leaders in faith communities, we are to make disciples, then what is our process for shaping them? Do we have a vision for discipling Christians with whom we work and serve (Ephesians 4:7-16)?

Figure 3.1 visualizes the catalytic role of the pastor/leader in shaping a reconciling and transforming congregation through "reaching up" in worship and devotion; "reaching out" through witness, service, or evangelism; "reaching in" through Christian nurture and spiritual discipline; and "reaching around" through fellowship and community through the Body of Christ, the People of God. This is the big picture and grand task of discipleship training. It is our vision. This represents the quality of believers we hope to develop.

Included in the vital component of dreaming and planning is the review of plans and programs that are designed to equip others for ministry and mission. Look around for resources to assist you as you seek to accomplish your goal. Begin to identify models that fit your local church, ministry organization, or college.

Visit denominational websites for discipleship programs. I am particularly impressed with the publication, *Nazarene Essentials: Who We Are — What We Believe, published by the Church of the Nazarene* and edited by Dr. Frank Moore (2015). The gifted editor discusses the Articles of Faith and the core values of the denomination and also provides a brief overview of Wesleyan theology.

Mobile apps are available to guide individuals and groups through Bible studies by books or themes of the Bible. One of the most helpful mobile apps is the YouVersion Bible application. Various versions of the Bible are provided for the readers. Also, numerous programs and plans for Bible reading and study provide access to entire books of the Bible, certain themes or seasons of the Christian year.

Some companies specialize in providing specific discipleship programs with materials available for shaping your community of faith for mission and ministry effectiveness. These companies are serious a b o u t providing individuals, churches, and small group discipleship and mission resources.

Do not overlook the Christian colleges, universities, and seminaries that often provide online short-term courses, academic programs, classes, and biblical and theological studies.

The Mesoamerica and South America Regions of the Church of the Nazarene, led by Regional Directors, Dr. Carlos Saenz, and Dr. Christian Sarmiento, with their regional education coordinators, Dr. Ruben Fernandez and Dr. Jorge Julca, have developed one of the best discipleship training programs in the Church of the Nazarene, from my perspective. Their program, Discipleship for Life, provides region-wide and cross-generation training programs for new and growing Christians from basic Bible and theological studies through ministerial education at the doctoral level.

The Mesoamerica and South America Regions provide systematic training on five levels of discipleship:

Level A: Pre-Conversion to Evangelism

Level B: Baptism to Church Membership

Level C: Sanctification, Living the Christian Life; and growth in holiness;

Level D: Ministry development and the School of Leadership;

Level E: Professional Ministerial Education and Careers in theological education.

In addition to discipleship study guides and classes for believers in local churches, the Regions offer academic programs in the "Bachillerato" in theology, as well as in the "Licenciatura" in theology. They also provide a diploma program in theological teaching. The Regions train pastor-professors for teaching in their decentralized education programs. A master's program and a doctoral program are available through the regional seminaries.

With an eye toward the future, the South America Region created a "Wesleyan Institute of Nazarene Identity," an intergenerational meeting point to preserve the Wesleyan theological heritage. The goal of this impressive, comprehensive discipleship program is to "Shape a new generation of Christian ministers in South America."

76

Dr. Monica Mastronardi de Fernandez, the general editor of the "ABCDE" Discipleship Program for the Mesoamerica Region, has written outstanding material for use at every level of the training model. The "ABCDE" series begins at the local church level. The general editor of the series, along with regional leaders and local church pastors, passionately believe that all Christians in every congregation must be trained and equipped in the basic concepts of Christian discipleship. The program contains numerous courses and rich resource materials.

You may feel as though the breath and depth of the Mesoamerica and South America Regions' training program is far out of your reach to duplicate, and you are probably right. The point in sharing their program is to illustrate how leaders in the Caribbean, Mexico, Central America, and in South America embraced a mission and vision for their responsibility group. In their case, that group was a combination of regions, a vast scope of land and people crossing economic and language divides. The complexity of their situation did not deter them from developing a plan to accomplish their mission and realize their vision. God is blessing the regions with phenomenal success in their discipleship-training program, which is available in Spanish, Portuguese, and English.

Not only did the Mesomerica and South America Regions begin with a discipleship model, they developed the plan and organized their resources to implement, administer, and train the teachers in the Discipleship for Life plan. More information is available about these discipleship programs through the regional education coordinators. The goal in Discipleship for Life is clear. Regardless of location, age, or size, for a community of faith to be equipped and shaped for mission and ministry, their leaders must be decisive and faithful in their leadership roles!

The leadership functions of dreaming and planning, administrating and organizing, motivating and inspiring, and evaluating and encouraging must take place with the big goal of nurturing and shaping disciples. Indeed, the leader is the catalyst in shaping a Christian fellowship or local church congregation into a reconciling and transforming community through "reaching up, reaching out, reaching in, and reaching around."

Establishing Growth *Goals* for Ministry and Mission

I remember teaching a course in organizational leadership several years ago and students began to ask questions, very basic questions, about goal setting in the context of ministry preparation. The following session, I returned to class, somewhat apologetically, with an outline.

At a very basic level, specific GOALS should:
1. Be measurable.
2. Be relevant.
3. Be attainable.
4. Contain an action verb.
5. Include a deadline. (David, 2011, p. 134)

The sharpest student in the class, with respect to me yet with firmness in his voice, said to me, "If you don't teach us these things, who will?"

Growth goals are *statements of faith* for the Christian leader that express clearly what we believe God will do through us.

Establishing goals and programs for equipping believers for ministry and mission to reach their goals and aspirations is not just for the regional or designated leaders of organizations. It also applies to leaders in Christian families and in local churches.

For instance, study the following goal statements. Using the five, basic criteria for establishing growth goals, identify the specific goal statement with the letter (S) and the vague goal statement with the letter (V)?

1.a. to have more people in services.
1.b. to increase participation in our mission and ministry programs by 20%.

2.a. to implement a financial campaign so we can build the facility debt-free.
2.b. to increase significantly the giving next year in our organization.

3.a. to challenge people to increase their financial giving.
3.b. to become a self-supporting ministry organization or congregation within two years.

4.a. to do a better job at communicating our ministry next year.
4.b. to spend at least 12 hours each week in person-to-person leadership development.

5.a. to start at least three classes or programs in the next 12 months.
5.b. to have more programs on our ministry organization.

6.a. to improve the appearance of our facility.
6.b. to repair and paint the after school program classrooms, the chapel or meeting room, and the organization sign during the next 12 months.

Several years ago, it was estimated that only a small percentage of all leaders actually write goals for themselves and for their leadership assignment. When I shared this percentage with a group of pastors recently, the group affirmed that, from their perspective, the figures were correct.

Please identify several specific goals, using the listed criteria, for the church, institution, or ministry organization you serve:

_____

_____

Strong goals motivate us, give us purpose, keep priorities straight, channel and maximize our potential, and promote enthusiasm in an organization. They help us operate more effectively, evaluate progress, plan ahead, and communicate. Goals take the emphasis off *activity* and place it on *results*.

Several years ago, I spoke at a conference on the broad subject of "Goal-Setting," and used the outline below to address the theme assigned to me. Following the presentation, I was curious with the responses to my question: Which one of the ten points relate most to your specific leadership assignments.

What would be your response? Why?

Leaders Who Make Things Happen

1. Leaders who make things happen are "deciders" rather than "drifters."

2. Leaders who make things happen know where they are going and how they are going to get there.

80

3. Leaders who make things happen are results-oriented and not activity-oriented.

4. Leaders who make things happen are among the small percentage who write down their growth goals.

5. Leaders who make things happen develop a mission statement as the foundation upon which every ministry of the district, region, or institution is built or evaluated.

6. Leaders who make things happen are dreamers who dream great dreams!

7. Leaders who make things happen understand leadership as the transference of vision!

8. Leaders who make things happen think big and dare to aim high by establishing growth goals that are measurable, feasible, attainable, and that have an action verb and a deadline.

9. Leaders who make things happen do not stop with writing down growth goals. They work hard at detailing programs and plans by which the goals will be reached.

10. Leaders who make things happen expect great things from God and attempt great things for God. They work as if it all depended on them and pray as if it all depended on God!

Equipping Others for Transitions and Tension

Not everyone you lead wants to change or to acknowledge that change is necessary. Change is inevitable in many situations—in the community, economy, demographics, expectations, technology, government, and education. Problems arise in the *transitions* related to these *inevitable* changes. Our equipping responsibility includes preparing others for transitions and the tensions that often follow.

Understanding transitions is important for the leaders and followers in the church or organization we serve. It helps us prepare those for whom we are responsible. It has a direct impact on our efficiency and mission effectiveness. Questions church leaders need to ask are: Do organizations and congregations (including individuals) go through numerical (and spiritual) cycles? Are the cycles inevitable? How do they regain momentum in the midst of cycles?

Bridges (1991) discussed transitions in the context of change and transitions. He believed that "In transition there is an ending, then a neutral zone, and only then a new beginning" (p. 70). He continued, "But those phases are not separate stages with clear boundaries. The three phases of transition are more like curving, slanting strata in any situation" (p. 70)

The sequence generally flows as follows:

- Someone has a dream.

- You slow down to resource your dream.

- The vision takes hold.

- The organization grows and is most effective and efficient.

- There is decline when the same things are done as in earlier years do not work.

- Time taken for a new vision. Breakout initiatives are needed.

- A turnaround vision is embraced. Leadership has responsibility to start a new, life-giving, phase.

Regarding the *old endings*, the leader must ask: What are the old endings that must go? What are the core values of the old that must be retained?

Regarding the *Transition* period, the leader's role is to articulate the *end* vision but retain core convictions. The leader during this period of change and transition must model consistency, steadiness, integrity, respect, trust, and communication.

Regarding *new beginnings*, the leader must engage the people in institutionalizing the transition through which they are going and toward which they are moving. The leader must continue to model the Christian character qualities of Ephesians 4 and I Peter 1, especially in conflict situations and with congregational members who differ with one another.

There is a critical time when the leader and board have the responsibility to both monitor and guide the phases. Additional questions leaders must ask themselves and their community include:

1. Where is organization in the cycle?

2. What should be the role of the ministry director/pastor in the cycle? board?

3. What should be the leader's specific role in transition phases?

In my inaugural address as president of Mount Vernon Nazarene College, I spoke on the subject of "Education for a Lifestyle of Service." I concluded my address by stating:

> *The next step for the MVNC faculty and administrators is to examine the implications of the ethic-of-service motif. We must explore together the implications of our commitment to a lifestyle of service as we review our general education core curriculum; develop seminars, conferences, workshops, and short-term modules for the Free Enterprise Business Center; consider nontraditional and degree-completion programs; enlarge continuing education opportunities on and off campus, and revise the field education and intern programs (see www.BoardServe.org/Writings. Scroll to Inaugural addresses).*

Financially, MVNC was a strong higher education institution, with reserves and annual balanced budgets and low debt. It was highly regarded for its education, pre-medicine, art, theology and Christian *ministry*, and business academic programs.

What I noticed was that the undergraduate enrollment had remained steady between 1000 and 1085 students for the previous five years. There were no graduate programs offered at the college and no extension campuses, when I began my presidency at MVNC.

Following *endless* faculty, staff, and administrative meetings, an engaged faculty (I was given a gift at my first faculty retreat of a cape with the words, "The Memo Man" written across the cape!) and an involved Board of Trustees, the undergraduate enrollment broke through the 1100 mark within two years. In addition, the first satellite campus site, offering an undergraduate business program in a non-traditional format, was in place within three years; and graduate programs were approved within four years. New buildings were constructed on campus within seven years either debt free or with very low debt, including a beautiful Library/Learning Resource Center, expanded student housing, enlarged dining commons, and additional academic facilities.

A two-year process studying the issue of moving the college to university level concluded with the Board of Trustees approving a recommendation to transition Mount Vernon Nazarene College to Mount Vernon Nazarene University. Within 15 years, the university had more than doubled its enrollment, more than tripled its annual operating budget, increased the campus size by over 40%, closed every year with a balanced budget, provided on-line academic program options, and nine satellite campuses in Ohio offering undergraduate and graduate academic programs.

A resolute commitment was evident to *equip and prepare* the campus community in the strategic plan *to accomplish the mission and vision* for MVNC. Ten years later, the College Board of Trustees created and approved an entirely new strategic plan to guide us as an institution into the new century. The institution responded to the need for a new vision, a big "break-out" initiative, as the college prepared for the 21st century. We took the growth and decline cycle seriously and worked collaboratively to manage the transitions well—most of the time!

"We must be captured by a vision,
which transcends ministry *to* the people,
and ministry *for* the people,
to ministry *with* and ministry *by* the people."
(Kinsler, 1983, p. 1)

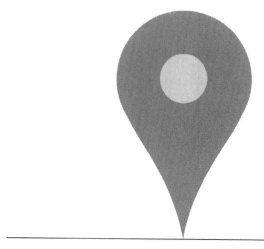

MARKER FOUR:

THE METHOD OF LEADING DECISIVELY IN ACCOMPLISHING THE VISION INCLUDES MENTORING, BOARD GOVERNANCE, MISSIONAL PLANNING, AND A ROBUST COMMUNITY.

Chapter Four

MARKER FOUR:
THE METHOD OF LEADING DECISIVELY IN ACCOMPLISHING THE VISION INCLUDES MENTORING, BOARD GOVERNANCE, MISSIONAL PLANNING, AND A ROBUST COMMUNITY.

Strong boards empower MISSIONAL and VISIONARY leaders;
Strong leaders embrace PASSIONATE and ENGAGED boards.
Edward LeBron Fairbanks

A "discipling" mentor communicates in word and deed that God is more interested in our character than our comfort. The character qualities God wants His people to demonstrate within the Christian community are further developed in II Peter 1:5-9:

For this very reason, make every effort to add to your faith goodness; and to goodness, knowledge; and to knowledge, self-control; and to self-control, perseverance; and to perseverance, godliness; and to godliness, brotherly kindness; and to brotherly kindness, love. For if you possess these qualities in increasing measure, they will keep you from being ineffective and unproductive in your knowledge of our Lord Jesus Christ. But if anyone does not have them, he is nearsighted and blind, and has forgotten that he has been cleansed from his past sins.

If the leader and the led possess these qualities, they will be productive and effective in their Christian walk and relationships. These character qualities parallel the qualities identified in Ephesians 4:2-3 — humility, gentleness, patience, supportiveness, and unity — and characterize followers of Christ who walk and lead worthy (cf. Ephesians 4:1) of their calling.

Constantly communicated by example more than by words is the truth that God wants for me to be available to Him, not to do things to prove I'm valuable to Him. "He is known as one who goes around doing good," affirmed Dr. Jim Bond, General Superintendent emeritus in the Church of the Nazarene, in reference to a colleague. A university president, on the retirement of a senior administrator at the university, stated, "He combined the twin attributes of intellectual competence and spirituality with a spirit of optimism and grace." What a compliment to an outstanding mentor and the mentee!

While working at the Global Ministry Center for the Church of the Nazarene, a friend applied for the Master of Divinity degree program at Northwest Nazarene University (NNU). A requirement for the graduate program was for the student to have a designated and approved mentor throughout the program. My friend asked me to serve in the role as his mentor. I agreed to the request, and we tried to meet at least monthly during the years of his M.Div. program. NNU required that I sign a contract agreeing to their expectations of a mentor to the student. It was a great experience for me. My friend and I continue to talk regularly.

During our sessions together, we would often return to basic mentoring questions, asked in different ways on different occasions:

How can we more consistently relate our testimony of holiness of heart and life to the way we live and lead in the home, on the job, and in the local congregation? Do those in the faith community closest to us witness consistently a reconciled and reconciling holiness lifestyle?

When were we at our best (or most effective) since we last met? What characterized us in those moments?

When and where were we at our worst (or least effective)? Why, and why here?

Other questions we discussed in the mentor or mentored relationship included:

1. What kind of future do you envision for your life, family, congregation, or ministry organization?

2. What are your dreams for the group for which you are responsible?

3. How are you doing, personally?

4. How are you progressing in your ministry assignment?

5. How can I help you?

In any mentoring relationship, discussions frequently take place around ongoing mistakes of an emerging leader (Table 4.1):

Table 4.1. Ongoing Mistakes of an Emerging Leader.

Mistakes	Necessary Alternatives
1.	1.
2.	2.
3.	3.
4.	4.
5.	5.
6.	6.
7.	7.
8.	8.
9.	9.
10.	10

A good question to ask a future leader who tends to talk rather continuously about the problems with little attention to possible solutions is, "Therefore, what...?"

As a mentor, begin to define the areas in your mentee that need attention. Using Table 4.1 as a starting point, look at specific issues.

To help you develop a mentoring process, you may want to develop your own list of mentoring questions based on the questions, which I, periodically, asked the leadership team at MVNU:

1. *Why* do you work at this ministry organization?

2. Have you matured in your faith as a result of your work?

3. Do your *spiritual gifts* match the responsibilities assigned to you?

4. Where do you feel most *vulnerable* or weak?

5. What are *your* core values of living and working in a faith community?

6. What can we do to strengthen and articulate your core values?

7. How are you working to more effectively communicate the mission and vision to the colleagues with whom you work most closely and those employees in your administrative division?

8. What questions do you have for me?

9. How can I assist you to increase your effectiveness in leading those for whom you are responsible?

10. What would you like for me to consider or change in my leadership role at MVNU?

Often, I re-frame these questions to people for whom I continue to feel a keen mentoring responsibility. Mentoring agendas differ vastly according to need, purpose, time, money and personnel. However, the more structured the plan or strategy, the better chance there is for sustained growth of the mentored. Be proactive — not reactive.

We often shift roles in the mentoring process. We mentor some individuals, and others, in turn, mentor us in other contexts.

While at MVNU, I created several advisory councils, with whom I met on a regular basis. I would ask a group of approximately 20 pastors from our region these questions:

1. What are you hearing (about MVNU) that I need to hear?

2. What are you thinking or dreaming about MVNU?

3. What are your concerns about this institution?

4. What new ideas would you like for me (or the campus leadership team) to consider?

5. What is the key issue facing your congregation today?

6. Since we face many of those same issues with students, how can we better work together to address these issues and concerns?

To another group I asked:

1. Is MVNU fundamentally the same school that it was when it was started in 1968? Is it the same place that founding President Stephen Nease spoke of in a letter to his mother, "We are having the time of our lives…convinced that we enjoy one of the rare opportunities ever found in the church"?

2. Are faculty, staff, and administrators working with the same sense of passion and purpose?

3. Am I the same president as when I moved to Mount Vernon?

4. Is "calling" to our specific assignment on campus still a word in our vocabularies and a conviction and reality in our hearts?

5. When was the last time we had a "burning bush" experience on campus?

In retirement, I meet regularly with two other men, whom I admire and respect greatly. We meet face to face, communicate by Facebook and by e-mail, and send each other material we are writing or share thoughts we are thinking.

Your "accountability group" or advisory group will differ from mine, as will your questions. However, as leaders, it is important for us to switch hats at appropriate times and be mentored by others. The question is not exclusively "Who are you mentoring? The question does include the parallel concern, "Who is mentoring you?" We are better and stronger leaders because we ask and listen.

Douglas Stone and Sheila Heen (2014), in their excellent book, *Thanks for the Feedback: The Science and Art of Receiving Feedback Well*, remind us that the feedback giver or mentor can help us see our blind spots when we are open to the question, "What do you see me doing, or failing to do, that is getting in my way" (p. 91)?

They also remind us that "feedback" is really three different things, with different purposes: "*Appreciation* — motivates and encourages; *Coaching* — helps increase knowledge, skill, capacity, growth, or raises feelings in the relationship; and *Evaluation* — tells you where you stand, aligns expectations, and informs decision making" (Stone Heen, 2014, p. 45).

All three are important but we often talk at cross-purposes (Stone & Heen, 2014, p. 45). For the mentor and the mentoree, we are encouraged to "be thoughtful about what you need and what you're being offered, and get aligned" (p. 45). Good advice!

A very basic tool to use and share with the person you are mentoring is the Pareto Principle, developed by John Maxwell (1993):

TWENTY PERCENT OF YOUR PRIORITIES WILL GIVE
YOU EIGHTY PERCENT OF YOUR PRODUCTION,
IF YOU SPEND YOUR
TIME, ENERGY, MONEY, AND PERSONNEL
ON THE TOP 20 PERCENT OF YOUR PRIORITIES.
(pp. 20-21)

WHAT ARE YOUR TOP TWO PRIORITIES?
SPEND 80% OF YOUR TIME ON THESE
TWO PRIORITIES.

Diligent Board Governance as Method

Early in my tenure at MVNU, I conducted my first local church board, two-day planning retreat. The format of our day together focused on "Characteristics of Strong and Effective Board Members."

In that retreat setting, I realized the mentoring role a leader had in relation to his/her governing board. Since that retreat years ago, I have given significant time studying both the characteristics of strong and effective boards of local congregations; ministry organizations; and colleges, universities, and seminaries. Implementation strategies propel pastors and ministry organization leaders toward intentionally mentoring and nurturing the boards they lead to be more efficient and effective for mission accomplishment.

1. It has been said that our lives can be characterized, summarized, and, perhaps, condensed into one sentence. Could the same be said of the governing board(s) on which we serve? I tend to agree.

2. If you agree, how would you characterize the most effective boards on which you serve...in one sentence?

   _____

3. Least effective?

   _____

STRONG BOARDS EMPOWER *MISSIONAL* AND *VISIONARY* PASTORS; STRONG LEADERS EMBRACE *PASSIONATE* AND *ENGAGED* BOARDS.

I shaped this statement over the years as I encountered strong boards and weak leaders and also the opposite—strong leaders and weak boards. It is not "either/or" for decisive leaders with a vision to serve; rather it must be "both/and."

Characteristics of strong and effective boards are listed in Appendix B. This section is developed more fully in a book, *Best Practices for Effective Boards,* which I co-authored with James Couchenour, and Dwight Gunter (2012). The book is available on Amazon for downloading.

Characteristic 1, "the role, purpose, and function of the board," is the overarching characteristic of healthy boards. If ignored, the remaining 11 characteristics and best practices will not be embraced. Maturing boards *focus on policy formulation and mission strategy; not daily operations and implementation.* Their "heads" are engaged with questions, observing, listening, and speaking; their "fingers" are not involved in the daily operations and implementation development of the strategy or policy.

How would you modify this list in Appendix B with additions or deletions to make these "characteristics" a mentoring outline to guide the work with your board? List below the top three "characteristics" and "best practices" for you and your board to focus on during the next six to eighteen months.

1. _____
2. _____
3. _____

Recently, I asked pastors and local church boards during a BoardServe tour to think about a local church board *vision* statement. I encouraged them to think about a statement that would give their boards a "big picture" of *why* they do what they do. Why do they work regularly on the seemingly routine and mundane work of a ministry organization or the local congregation? For what purpose? To what end do "our" efforts lead? What characterizes a board at its best? I suggested the following statement as a starting point:

"The leadership ministry of "our" church board *enables* church attendees to fulfill *their* ministry to each other, and the church's mission in the neighborhood and beyond."

How would you adapt this statement to the board on which you serve?

Do you "see" in the statement a way of boards "viewing" themselves and the work they do on a regular basis? What difference on your board would it make if the members viewed themselves as a leadership team, working with the pastor, to enable the congregation to serve others in Jesus' name? Everything that is done in a board meeting would intentionally serve to facilitate, equip, and enable the congregation in the Christian ministry to each other and their participation in the church's mission, which is really the mission of God, in your neighborhood and beyond!

"Govern diligently" (Romans 12:8c). The following devotional and board development presentation to the Asia-Pacific Nazarene Theological Seminary Board of Trustees has been modified for this book. Characteristics of effective board governance are addressed.

"We have different gifts; according to the grace given to us...If it is leadership, let him govern diligently" (Romans 12:6-8b NIV).

In the fascinating 12th chapter of Romans, two words speak to me as I think about governing boards of local churches, district and national boards, and the college, university, and seminary boards. The words from 12:8 are "govern diligently."

What does it mean to "govern diligently?" What is a "governing board?"

In my work with boards in various countries, I have found much ambiguity regarding board governance. Members want to make a positive impact on the boards to which they belong. They are thrilled to be asked to serve on a governing board.

For many, the invitation provides an opportunity to be good stewards of the gifts, talents, education, and experiences with which they have been blessed. Often, however, this excitement soon leads to frustration as the boards on which they serve lack an understanding of the role, purpose, and structure of the board.

The big question regarding governing boards is this: "What should a local church, ministry organization, or seminary governing board do to be a strong and effective board who "governs diligently...and effectively?"

In a YouTube video series on "Building Better Boards" (www.youtube.com, search for LeBron Fairbanks), I define a governing board as "...an elected body that oversees the ministry and mission of a local church or ministry organization between annual membership meetings." A governing board of a local church or a ministry organization "is guided by the Church Manual and/or ministry organization Bylaws and Articles of Incorporation," and must insure that the legal documents and policy documents are current.

Organizations, including local churches and ministry organizations, evolve and change, and so must their governing boards. Strong and effective boards receive recommendations from the church or organization membership; boards also shape strategic recommendations for the full membership to consider. *Strategic thinking, planning, and implementation are key responsibilities of a governing board* that "governs diligently."

Review the modified Sigmoid or "S" curve. Understanding this cycle is critical for boards to govern the organization for sustained growth. Change is inevitable; problems arise in the transitions.

It is a proper management of the problems and the change that will determine if this organization and the people in it will be successful.

The vertical line on the left in Figure 4.1 represents the "growth" line. The horizontal line at the bottom of the slide represents the "timeline" and can represent weeks, months, or years. If organizations, including churches, continue to function as they did at the start of the local church or beginning of the ministry organization, then the growth will subside, and decline will begin. New "breakout" initiatives and vision are needed along the timeline (A), even as growth is taking place! If not, the church or organization will soon plateau and eventually decline (B)!

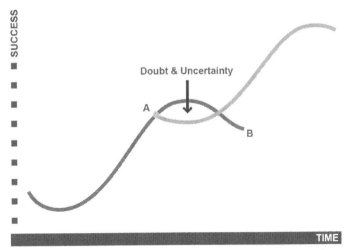

SUCCESS

Doubt & Uncertainty

A

B

TIME

Figure 4.1. Modified "S" Curve for Asia-Pacific Nazarene Theological Seminary Governing Board.

This board development segment focuses on the Asia-Pacific Nazarene Theological Seminary governing board. Together, the board needs to consider questions like this one: What *new* initiatives need to take place to increase the influence and impact of APNTS throughout the region and *to insure continued growth* in the seminary enrollment?

Remember, change is inevitable — change in demographics, expectations, economics, technology, government, and education — just to name a few. Problems arise in the transitions. How *do* we adjust to the facts, context, and trends we face in the changing community, country, or region in which we work and serve?

Understanding transitions is important for the boards and the board chairs or leaders. The "Sigmoid Curve" helps us conceptualize inevitable change and necessary transitions in the higher education institutions, local churches, or ministry organizations with whom we serve.

Additional questions to be asked by the governing board and the seminary leadership included:

1. Do graduate level theological seminaries go through numerical (and spiritual) cycles? Are the cycles inevitable? How do these schools regain momentum in the midst of cycles?

2. Where is the seminary in the cycle?

3. What should be the role of board and seminary leadership in this cycle, particularly at the transition points?

How we manage the transitions can *facilitate* or *derail* the influence, impact, and the enrollment growth of the seminary. Remember the foundational working assumption regarding my perspective on governing boards of faith organizations, especially local churches and college and seminary boards.

"Strong Governing Boards Empower Effective Leaders; Strong Leaders Embrace Engaged Boards."

Growing local churches, ministry organizations, and schools like the Asia-Pacific Nazarene Theological Seminary need strong and effective governing boards in order to identify new initiatives and to create a fresh and relevant vision for the seminary. Otherwise, decline will be the result.

Healthy boards engage board members. They ask thoughtful questions but do not attempt to micro-manage the organization. They respect their ministry organization leader, seminary president, or local church pastor. As an effective governing board, they have nominated or elected the very strongest, mission *fit leaders* possible. These leaders know, communicate, make decisions, and submit recommendations to the board with a laser-beam commitment to the organization's mission, vision, and values. They have earned the trust of their boards and work in cooperation with them.

Likewise, strong leaders "lead" by bringing out the best in board members, listening to them and providing significant opportunities for them to *engage* in the decision-making process. These leaders are not intimidated by probing questions. They take time to process questions in need of answers and challenges in need of decisions. They guard against "intentional" surprises by board members or board leaders. These leaders model a commitment to communicate with each other and address conflict situations as Christians.

Four "Modes of Thinking"

To lead and be effective as a governing board means to function appropriately in the four modes of board governance: the FIDUCIARY mode; the STRATEGIC mode, the REPRESENTATIVE mode, and the REFRAMING mode. These four modes of thinking and governance may be briefly summarized as follows:

Fiduciary mode. The word, "fiduciary" is a legal term. Its goal is to insure the legal and financial integrity of the organization. Being a fiduciary implies that the board serves as a steward of the mission and the future of the organization and its tangible assets. This mode insures that appropriate audits are performed and focuses on issues such as Articles of Incorporation, By-laws, Required Government Documents, Payroll, and Insurance documentation, Property, Ethics and integrity, Legal, and Financial compliance, Board minutes, and mission clarity.

Strategic mode. In this mode of thinking, the board serves as planning partner with the church, college, or ministry organization leader. Being "strategic" implies that the board is proactive and intentional in long-term planning for the organization. The board does not necessarily prepare the strategic plan for the organization but assures that one is current and serving as a roadmap for the future. This mode focuses on mission, vision, priorities, strategic initiatives, timeline, personnel, and budget.

Representative mode. This mode of thinking reflects the thinking of the moral owners of the organization. The "representative" thinker especially appreciates the heritage of the church, college, or ministry organization. This mode of thinking serves as the "guardian" of values in the organization. In this mode of thinking, the board remembers why the organization was founded and seeks to "conserve" the organization's founding purpose. History is important to the "representative."

Reframing mode. This mode of thinking seeks to "reframe" the presenting problem and "make sense" of the issues by connecting the dots. The "reframer" tries to identify the big picture or issue and seeks to serve as a problem-framer. Often, this mode of thinking will attempt to re-envision the situation with implications for the future. Thinking in this mode often compels the board to restate the presenting problem in a "big-picture" context.

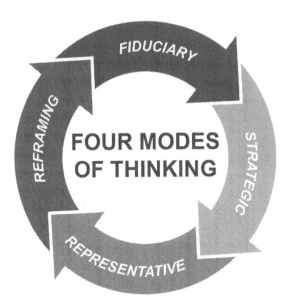

Figure 4.2. Four modes of thinking. © E.L. Fairbanks

Increasingly, I am convinced that healthy and maturing boards have a balance in board membership between the four modes of thinking (see Figure 4.2) about board governance: fiduciary, strategic, representative, and reframing. When boards are comprised of a predominance of one of these four modes of thinking, the board and organization suffer. Most of us serving on boards would like to think that we are strong in all four areas. Not so! The board needs people who are strong in different areas to insure that the balance required for healthy and maturing boards is present. We prefer to serve with people who think and act like us! One sure sign of a strong board is when one member says to another, "I don't understand what you are saying, but I think it is important, and I need to listen to your perspective. Help me understand."

In Figure 4.2, the model of the "Four Modes..." (Fairbanks) clearly indicates the cyclical relationship of this way of thinking in board meetings. It is not linear in nature. Issues can arise in any of the four areas. Important, however, is that these four dimensions, expressed appropriately with civility, care, and a "laser-beam" commitment to the organization's vision, most often bring out the best in the board and provide for a more thoughtful, collective response to the agenda issue.

This means that the board has governance and coordinating responsibility for the seminary, ministry organization, or local congregation in at least the areas of:

- Mission and Vision clarity

- Financial health and legal standing

- Budget approval and oversight

- Problem-framing and "sense-making"

- Curriculum consistency

- Doctrinal integrity

- Spiritual well-being of the congregation, ministry organization or students

- Strategic thinking, planning and implementation oversight.

Let's go deeper by asking several additional questions:

1. What *one* word would you use to characterize this board?

2. What are the major strengths of this board?

3. What is the most *critical issue or major concern* facing this board?

4. What *board-related question* would you like answered during board meeting?

5. Are the *legal documents* up to date, and readily available to board members?

6. What three *big ideas* should the Board focus on for the next three years?

7. What has *changed* significantly in the community surrounding the seminary, organization, or local church to which the board must adjust and make appropriate transitions?

These *big questions* can only be asked and thoughtfully discussed if the board agenda has been intentionally developed. Guard the board agenda! Significant reports are important and so are the blocks of time needed to discuss the big questions facing the church, ministry organization, or seminary.

Don't back away from the big questions. Cultivate the discipline to construct *think questions* — not just any questions. Strong and effective boards ask the *right* questions. The previous seven questions are examples of basic, on-going questions that probe the big issues and help define the real problems.

Governing boards will shape the specific questions needed for a particular time and setting. Boards may not have immediate answers to the fiduciary, strategic, representative or reframing challenges before them. Boards must, however, have the right questions. And, in this process, they increasingly "govern diligently."

Lifespan and stages of a faith community. Change is inevitable; and churches, college, seminaries, and ministry organizations must embrace constant change. Problems arise in the transitions. How do we adjust to the facts, context, and trends we face in the changing community or country in which we work and serve?

Lifespan and stages of a Faith Community

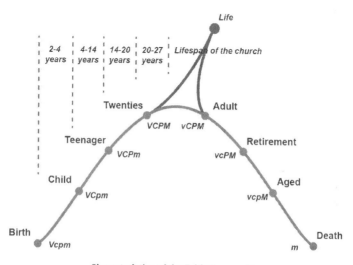

Figure 4.3. Lifespan and stages of a faith community. (Inspired by Dale, 1981, pp. 15, 17, 19, 26, 115)

Where is the organization you serve "located" on the curve? Notice the "characteristics" of a faith community at the bottom of Figure 4.3. Pay particular attention to the capital VCPMs. Where are they the strongest (represented by capital letters)? Weakest? Vision indeed does drive new congregations, churches, businesses, and ministry organizations.

In his book, *Deep Change: Discovering the Leader Within*, author Robert Quinn (1996) explores the dynamic process of deep change and learning the new ways of thinking and behaving. The radical choice he places before us as the organizations we lead enter their "adulthood" is to "face the deep change or slow death dilemma" (p. 96).

It is when things seem to be going well (represented by the capital letters VCPM) that faith communities and ministry organizations are tempted to say, "Look how far we have come, why change now?" It is with this mindset that organizations tend to plateau, level off, and experience doubt and uncertainty. It is precisely in the growth times when new initiatives, fresh vision, and creative plans need to come forth.

If not, then, decline is inevitable. The further the decline, the more radical the intervention needed to experience new life and continued growth as an organization.

Jim Collins (2009) believes that decline can be avoided. It can be detected and reversed. In his book, *How the Mighty Fall*, he uncovers five stages of decline:

Stage 1: Hubris Born of Success
Stage 2: Undisciplined Pursuit of More
Stage 3: Denial of Risk and Peril
Stage 4: Grasping for Salvation
Stage 5: Capitulation to Irreverence or Death (p. 20)

He believes that great organizations and companies can stumble and recover.

Strong boards and strong leaders have the potential to guide the organization to "break out" of the routine, and, even in decline, to discover new approaches to the new realities facing the church, school, or ministry organization. Asking good questions is critical to this turnaround.

Strategic Questions As Method

This section builds on the assumption that outstanding boards shape effective leaders and outstanding leaders embrace strong boards. The assumption requires that both leader and board ask the *right* questions of each other. Only then will strategic decision-making take place.

In candor, for this assumption to work itself out in the leader/board relationship, *Christian maturity and mutual respect* are required. *Christian convictions* about leading and being led will be evidenced as the policy-shaping and decision-making process of governing boards is experienced.

Stone and Heen (2014) challenged the readers to focus on change from the inside out (p. 95). They believe that "relationship triggers" may be the most common "derailers" of feedback conversations (p. 102).

Local churches and other Christian organizations expect that the members of the governing boards *are mature and deeply committed Christians. They* deserve board members who can engage each other on the board and advisory committees with penetrating questions about working together effectively and efficiently for mission and vision accomplishment.

It is possible that the very *functions* of boards can nurture transformative, redemptive, and reconciling relationships within and between board members.

Good questions - honest questions - first questions.
"What do board members do? How do board members do
what they do?" How do board members know what they are
supposed to do?"

Members of various boards will perhaps answer
these questions differently depending upon the nature of
the organization. Local church board members, for
instance, will respond to these questions differently than
members of college boards or community not-for-profit
boards, like the local YMCA board or community service
organization board.

In a cross-country airplane trip, a discussion ensued
regarding not-for-profit governing boards. One
participant in the conversation was reading a book on
board development. The other was the chief training and
development officer for a large insurance firm and an
officer in the national governing board for training and
developing professionals. The senior officer was asked,
"What is the mission of the professional governing board
on which you serve? What is the vision for the
organization? Is there a strategic plan for the national
organization that has been approved by the governing
board?"

A fascinating discussion continued, until the plane
landed in a major West Coast city. The senior officer could
not state the mission or define the vision for the
organization. There was *no* strategic plan. She wanted a
copy of the book on board development!

Board members know and communicate the mission,
vision, and values of the church, school, or not-for-profit
organization. They ask good questions that lead to strong
policies and decision-making with a laser-beam commitment
to the organization's mission, vision, and values.

Strong and effective boards think and work in four modes of governance. Let's review.

Responsibility #1: Fiduciary. Fiduciary responsibility requires that boards ask appropriate questions at critical junctures in the life of the organization. Questions such as, "Is a capital campaign or major gifts ramp up needed and trained fund raising consultants engaged to guide the board through the strategic project?" "Is a realistic operating budget in place?" "Are resources wisely used?"

Fiduciary responsibilities ensure that legal and financial integrity is maintained. Are the results monitored? Is due diligence pursued? College boards, for instance, exercise their fiduciary responsibility for the financial health, academic integrity of the college, and the spiritual well-being of the students who study and the employees who work at the school. These are board leadership questions.

Responsibility #2: Strategic. This mode of thinking requires a close working relationship with the pastor, staff, congregation, and the board or the appropriate parallels in ministry organizations. How is the plan designed, communicated, and modified? Are we proactive and intentional in strategic planning? Does the operating budget reflect the priorities of the strategic plan adopted by the board?

Responsibility #3: Representative. The representative mindset is rooted in the values, traditions, and beliefs of the local church, school, or organization. Problems are stated in light of the heritage of the institution. Does this program reflect the values of the denomination? For instance, "How does this expenditure facilitate in the making of Christ-like disciples in our community? How is the ethos of the college communicated through the academic programs? Are the

111

decisions violating the values of the college? Community organizations frame appropriate parallel questions.

Board members are representatives in two ways. They bring issues from the broader membership of the organization to the leader, and they reinforce the mission and vision of the leadership and board to broader membership.

Responsibility #4: Reframing. This mode of thinking seeks to *reframe* the presenting problem. "What is the *real* question?" "What is the big issue with which we are working?" This mode of thinking attempts to re-envision the situation with implications for the future. Thinking in this mode often compels the board to restate the presenting problem.

Board members ask *good* questions that lead to strong fiduciary, strategic, representative, and reframing policies and decision making with a resolute commitment to the mission, vision, and values of the organization.

Sense-making and problem-framing questions address the legal, planning, and restorative concerns of the faith community for which the board is responsible. These questions enable the board to make sense of the issues before them and to frame the problems in ways that bring focus and intentionality to the discussions.

Visional questions that help us identity issues and clarify the missional purpose of the local church are similar to a journalist's foundational questions for any report: who, what, where, when, and how. Asked another way, we probe these questions:

- Who are we?
- Where are we?

- Where are we going?
- How will we get there?
- Why is it important to get there?
- How will we know when we get there?
- What is the *real* issue?
- What is the CORE question?

When national education boards and regional accrediting agencies visit colleges and universities to review and evaluate the institutions and/or specific academic program areas, they ask the right questions. Although asked differently by various evaluators, the questions revolve around these categories of inquiries:

1. **Mission statement:** Does your school have a mission statement that is known, owned, and repeated? Is it the filter through which every policy and decision is screened? Is there overwhelming evidence of the connection between mission, policies, and programs?

2. **Resources:** Have you marshaled the resources to fulfill the mission? Do you have a balanced operating budget that is mission driven? Are human and financial resources dedicated to mission critical personnel and programs?

3. **Tracking and assessment:** Are you accomplishing your mission? What is your product? What is the quality of students you produce?

4. **Sustaining growth:** Are you going to marshal the resources to continue fulfilling your mission? Do you have a plan to sustain and develop the financial resources needed by the school to fulfill its mission?

Guarding the agenda. Shape the board agenda as appropriate to receive committee reports. The board agenda should be developed intentionally by planning significant time during the board meetings for regular, purposeful discussion of key questions. Some boards structure their meetings around three broad categories: information, discussion, and decision.

The items for discussion are each stated in the form of a *question*. This discipline helps focus the discussion on the real questions being considered.

Good questions can lead to a strong synergistic partnership between the board and the pastor, school leader, or organization leader. Board members *vigorously* discuss policy options and make decisions *within* the board meetings and communicate board action *outside* board meetings with a *unified* voice. This kind of relationship is like a good marriage. It is based on mutual respect, trust, commitment, effective communication... and good questions asked both ways. Questions like:

1. How would we define the "ethos" of our local church or organization?

2. What are we thinking or dreaming about the church or school?

3. What did we learn of greatest value this year?

4. What are we hearing that the pastor or the school/organizational administrators needs to hear?

5. What should we be worrying about as a local church, Christian college, or ministry organization?

6. What is success — given our congregational or institutional mission, vision, and values? What outcome do we desire? What is the end goal?

7. What are the concerns you hear expressed about the governing board?

8. What's going on?

9. What do you need me to do, if I am to be more effective as your leader?

10. What questions do we need to ask to better understand the overarching problem we are facing?

When you engage these questions or topics, boards are freed from *non-substantive* issues. The important questions are asked and thoughtfully, prayerfully, and honestly discussed. A stronger bond between pastor/leader and board is developed. There is less micro-management and more macro-management, more leading and less managing.

A fusion of thinking is the result. Both leader and board are forthcoming. Both accept a greater measure of responsibility for the policy decisions. The board meetings are more substantive and focused on the strategies needed for the mission and vision implementation as opposed to the drudgery of just managing the organization.

Forge together new directions for the future as opposed to dwelling on the past. Honestly address significant problems. Focus on solutions. Make decisions and insure implementation. Align resources. Create action plans in consultation with the leader/pastor. Both leader/pastor and the board are energized when they move in the same direction.

Strategic questions in crisis situations. Philosopher and educator John Dewey believed that a problem well defined was a problem half solved. In other words, work to clarify the *real* problem or issue that is creating the misunderstanding.

Crises sometimes arise within the life of a congregation or ministry organization. Asking good questions is essential for these crisis situations to be addressed properly, for the relationships within the board to mature, and for the work of the board to be effective. Strong leaders are not afraid of tough questions from the board and to the board during these times of crisis — questions that look back, evaluate the present, and anticipate the future.

Relational questions that need to be asked. As you think of the people with whom you work on the board, whom do you have the most difficulty accepting? What kinds of people are hardest for you to accept? Why do you think this is so? How do you think God sees that person — or those persons? How does your response affect your own relationship to God?

Pastors, school leaders, and organization directors often work with their governing boards in the creative and growth-producing tension of holding to a vision for the future, while holding just as firmly to the realities of the present, including board members who differ, and often collide, with the leader. In the *process* of working through this tension, *the leader and the board can experience the transforming, redemptive, and reconciling work of God in their relationships.* What a powerful witness to believers and non-believers.

116

Reflect on these *practical* lessons as you work together as a board to "accept one another, then, just as Christ accepted you, in order to bring praise to God" (Romans 15:7).

1. Good and godly people often see things differently.

2. Many issues over which we experience conflict are culturally, ethnically, local community, even family-based, and not a violation of scripture.

3. Differences that divide us have the potential to alienate members of the body of Christ and to impact negatively the actual and perceived work of God.

4. Respecting those who differ with us is to love them, as God loves them.

5. Acceptance of others implies that we can learn from them.

The overarching question is this: How can we *mature* in Christlikeness and increasingly reflect an acceptance of others (Romans 15:7) within the community of faith we serve, as we function with integrity and grace as a governing board?

Construct think questions---not just any questions. Each board will shape the specific questions needed for a particular time and setting. Boards may not have immediate answers to the fiduciary, strategic, representative or reframing challenges before them as a governing board. They must, however, have the right questions.

Missional Planning As Method

Over the years I have come to see that it is best to bring my very best thoughts to the board (or committee) and seek their involvement in the further development of the plan. Indeed, the plan will most likely be changed, but it will also be improved.

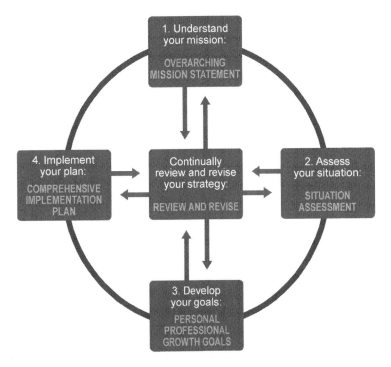

Figure 4.4. Planning cycle model. © E.L. Fairbanks

The planning cycle model (Figure 4.4) places the "review and revise" planning component in the center of the process. It is always appropriate to seek feedback as the leader strives to clarify the mission of the organization, assess the situation, develop appropriate goals, and develop an implementation strategy. Healthy boards do not hesitate to review policies, plans, and programs of the past, including fund development programs, that perhaps worked in previous years. Do not be paralyzed or frozen regarding current places or programs that need to be revised in order to move to a new level of organizational effectiveness and sustainability.

A three-year, board approved plan should include the components in Figure 4.4 with input from various stakeholders and with as much detail, as possible.

A missional plan provides leaders and boards the basis for replying with an emphatic "yes" or a regrettable "no," when suggestions are made as to new directions for the church or organization. Mission and vision are the keys. Stay focused on them. Good ideas may be rejected because they do not fit into the strategic plan of the local church, district, or ministry organization.

Flow of situation assessment process. In these and other areas of board responsibility, the board is a vital planning partner with the pastor/leader. Together you move from vision to action to results with clear vision, deep humility, and intense resolve. Consider using a strategic planning template as you prayerfully and with conviction begin to move from vision to action to results (see Appendix C).

Do not overlook the critical importance of systematically assessing the situation wherein your local church or ministry organization is located. Figure 4.5 enables the leader to ask the key questions regarding the organization's environment.

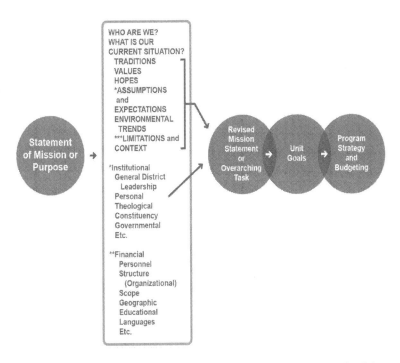

Figure 4.5. Flow of situation assessment process. (Modified by E.L. Fairbanks)

Planning strategically compels the leaders and followers to focus intentionally with an intense commitment to the mission and vision of the congregation or organization. Strategic planning is not exclusively "implementation" strategy. Rather the beginning point in planning strategically is to clarify and embrace the mission, vision, and values with the board to which the leader is accountable. Clarify the core "driving forces." Seek understanding. Define strategic initiatives and goals. Include personnel needs. Include financials and timelines. Seek ownership of the plan by the board. The key idea is for the missional plan to outline in detail the strategies by which the church or organization will accomplish the mission and realize the vision.

We discussed briefly in the previous chapter the importance of establishing growth goals. Remember that growth goals are statements of faith for the Christian leader that express clearly what we believe God will do through us. Goals are dreams with a deadline.

Happy is the person who dreams great God-inspired dreams, spends the appropriate time in assessing the situation or context, sets the appropriate goals to reach the dreams, and is willing to pay the price to see those dreams come true.

Edward LeBron Fairbanks

Legal and program audit. Resources and templates are available to assist the leader as s/he mentors and guides the congregation and board toward ministry and mission effectiveness. The APEX Project is an excellent example of the numerous resources available through denominational headquarters, para-church organizations, and companies designed to assist not-for-profit organizations and local churches. You can also access this *legal and program audit* at www.usacanadaregion.org/apex-organizational-assessment.

The APEX Project enables higher education leaders, organization directors, church pastors, and board chairpersons to conduct *legal and program audits* on the schools, companies, or churches they lead in the United States. (Adapt as necessary the instrument to use outside the USA.)

Categories include:
I.   Legal Documentation Checklist
II.   Mission/Vision/Values/Strategic Planning
III.   Board Development
IV.   Financial Accountability
V.   Fund Development
VI.   Human Resources

VII. Program Development
VIII. Organizational Capacity
IX. Priorities for Capacity Building

For instance, for the category of "Legal Documentation," on a scale of 1 to 4, the leader identifies the organization's level of compliance in areas as:

I. Articles of Incorporation
II. Bylaws
III. 501(c3) Status
IV. Payroll Documentation
V. IRS 990 Form
VI. Insurance Legal/Financial Advisors
VII. Registered Agent and Current Contact Address

For sure, not every item identified in the "Legal Documentation" category will apply equally toward all non-profit organizations. Some states may require additional information from the organization. However, the APEX Project is an excellent start on a legal and program audit.

If interested in the APEX Project, go to the website, www.usacanadaregion.org/apex-organizational-assessment. Click the words, "APEX Assessment" in the menu column, then the APEX Quick Reference Guide or the "Blank APEX Assessment Form.

I believe you will find the APEX Project a useful tool for faith-based organizations or non-governmental organizations and nonprofits who want to assess their organizational effectiveness and development opportunity. The instrument will also help organizations to identify areas of organizational capacity and to prioritize the areas that need strengthening.

The BoardServe DIAGNOSTIC instrument (Appendix D) is a beneficial tool and may be used as an alternative to the APEX Project in conducting a legal and program audit for their local churches.

Missional planning and board evaluation. Healthy and maturing boards include systematic board development and evaluation as an essential component of their missional planning. For board development to be effective, boards (a) make board development intentional; (b) focus on felt needs of the board; (c) include board development as a priority of the board agenda; (d) utilize book chapters and video links to assist the board; (e) find expertise needed to assist the board in key areas from within the congregation, Christians in other congregations, business and government leaders, and from not-for-profit organizations.

Do not overlook the periodic process of a board evaluation. Templates are available and must fit the specific board and context. You can modify the Board Evaluation Survey (Appendix E) to fit your particular board and congregation/organization. Answering these questions will provide for the board some specific answers for growth and development. Secure a consultant, as necessary, to provide guidance to the board or congregation as you work through the process, evaluate the results, and establish an action plan for board development.

Appendix E is similar to the BoardServe Diagnostic instrument, yet, different in the board's attempt to evaluate its own efficiency and effectiveness before asking the broader congregation or membership to evaluate them.

Both board members and board leaders, including pastors, completed the survey prior to our sessions together and returned the instrument to the consultant. The information is used in shaping the evening sessions to their specific questions and needs. The survey provided significant feedback, as the consultant attempted to evaluate the gap between the perceptions of board members with those of the board leader/chair.

Review of the leader. Accountability also includes the leader being reviewed periodically and especially prior to a renewal vote. From my own experience with a Board committee, I recognize that these occasions have the potential of generating some anxiety. Yet, our approach to the person reviewed should always be one of hope: for strengthening overall effectiveness and increasing efficiency in specific work assignments; for setting goals for personal and professional development; and for spiritual growth and new or improved ministry opportunities as a result of serving. Both as individuals and as a community, these times are necessary and valuable for cultivating our commitment to excellence for Christ (Colossians 3:23).

Reviewing the College principal prior to the vote of the College Board on an extension of his contract, a College Board reviewed the principal utilizing the Leader Effectiveness Review (see Appendix F). With other colleges, organization, or congregations, the title used for the leader is mandated in the institution's by-laws. Modifications of this template is available and should be adopted to meet the particular organization, board, and leader reviewing and being reviewed.

Mr. James LaRose founded the National Development Institute in 1991, to nurture and leverage philanthropy by supplying funders and organizations the capacity-building research and education to advance the missions of the organizations they serve. Mr. LaRose expanded his original dream to provide counselor/consultants and nonprofit organizations the professional expertise to raise major gifts for education, healthcare, human welfare, the arts, the

124

environment, and for local church ministry and mission.

The Major Gift Ramp-up Model. The Major Gifts Ramp-Up model is impressive in scope and also in resourcing leaders for implementing the system in nonprofit organizations of any size. Check these websites:

www.MajorGiftsRampUp.com
www.nationaldevelopmentinstitute.com
www.NonprofitConferencea.org
www.ConsultingCertification.org
www.JimmyLaRose.com

At a recent Major Gifts Ramp-Up conference on the campus of Mount Vernon Nazarene University, Mr. LaRose worked through the model (Figure 4.6), which is included here with permission from NDI (Appendix G).

The founder and CEO of the National Development Institute reminded the executives of nonprofit organizations and their board members that not-for-profit organizations were in two businesses: (1) providing a service; and (2) generating revenue necessary to provide the service. The conference theme focused on enabling these organizations to significantly raise the revenue needed to accomplish their organizational missions.

I was impressed with the Major Gifts Ramp Up model developed by Mr. Larose and taught by him and his faculty at National Development Conferences. His goal was not only to equip nonprofit boards, executives, staff, and volunteers with the training to implement a capital campaign required to sustain the organization's mission and vision but also to assist them through a very structured approach to complete the fundraising initiative successfully. With the key word being "equip," he not only

125

saw a need and had a dream on how to address the need but also developed a comprehensive strategy and implementation plan to move from vision, to action, to results.

Figure 4.6. Major Gifts Ramp-Up model.
Reprinted with permission (see Appendix G)

My segment of the conference was a presentation on "Five 'Non-negotiables' for Board Health and Fund Development." The focus was on organizational and board development as essential for major gifting for an organization. The stronger the organizational development of the organization, including strong and effective boards, the easier it is to build a *compelling* case for support of the organization.

Non-negotiables for Board Health and Fund Development

The "Board Health and Fund Development" presentation centered on key components in this chapter. Healthy and Maturing Boards:

1. **Know the basics.** Board members understand the essentials of the Board's role, purpose, and function. They focus on policy formulation and mission strategy, not on daily operations and implementation. These boards know that a governing board (a) oversees the mission; (b) develops a shared vision; and (c) shapes the future of the organization. Their number one responsibility is to *select* the best executive director possible for the organization; and their number two responsibility is to ensure organization's accountability…to the government, to the moral owners of the organization; and to provide accountability *for the leader(s)*.

2. **Ask the 'right' questions.** They nurture a culture of asking mission-driven and sustainability questions. Questions like *"Who are we?"* What are our mission, vision, and values? *Where are we?* This does not refer to a location on a map but the *lifespan* of the organization. *Where are we going* (if we continue to do as we have done)? *Where could we go* (with a Spirit-inspired vision and a unified board)? *Why are we going "there"?* What is our motivation for growth? *How long will it take to get there?* What are the spiritual, human, financial resources needed? How will we know when we get there? *What has changed* significantly in the community to which the board must adjust and make appropriate transitions? *What one thing*, if

we do not attend to this issue soon, *could create serious problems for us* in the near future? *What fresh revenue- generating options are available* to us to significantly increase revenue? *How can the MGRU model for fund development impact our organization?*

3. **Communicate in conflict situations with civility.** Collisions occur over vision, values, traditions, plans, or programs and...! Healthy and maturing board members vigorously discuss policy options and make decisions within board meetings. Once decisions are made, they communicate the board action outside of board meeting with unified support — no "minority" reports permitted. Confidential conversations are kept confidential. Acceptance of board decisions is a given. And, board members do what they say they will do, and not do. It is in conflict situations that we reflect our character. Our responses characterize us at our best and convict us at our worse.

4. **Embrace assessment of prior board decisions in light of present realities.** Healthy boards review and revise, as necessary, decision-making in shaping financial and organizational development strategies. Organizational leaders tend to believe that they must have the "plan" for a new fund development program "perfect" before they present it to their boards. Then, when "fresh" eyes look at the plan and see gaps, weakness or big questions unanswered, the leader is offended as if to say, "How can you say that? You have just seen it, and I have worked weeks (or months) on this plan!"

5. **Connect board decision-making to capacity building and organizational sustainability.** Map a compelling CASE FOR SUPPORT through forward-looking board policies. An up-to-date policy board *manual* is important. It should state clearly in an organized and understandable way the board-approved policies for effective legal, financial, and policy governance process and procedures of the organization. An up-to-date policy manual keeps the board from "knee-jerk" reactions, erratic and inconsistent actions, and poor decision-making strategies. A policy manual or organization handbook includes board policies and procedures in a notebook, which is provided to every board member and updated after each board meeting.

New boards can begin by developing their by-laws for governance. Older boards can insure that the by-laws are current. Once the bylaws are updated, begin to collect the board policies in an organized manner.

Money follows a well-articulated and thoughtfully prepared vision and plan. People also give to organizations where integrity, credibility, honesty, stewardship, consistency, and communication are more than slogans or tailgates of the organization. Rather the board lives out these qualities in and through their decision-making for the organization. They make decisions with a laser-beam commitment to the organization's mission, vision, and values.

The board standing policy manual. The manual or handbook may have as few as four pages but not more than 16 to 20 pages. The Board Standing Policy Manual in Appendix H outlines all of the standing or ongoing policies adopted by the Board of Governance for the organization, congregation, or institution.

Robust Community as Method

"Two are better than one, because they have a good reward for their toil. For if they fail, and one falls, one will lift up the other; but woe to one who is alone and falls and does not have another to help...two will withstand... a three-fold cord is not quickly broken" (Ecclesiastes 4:9-12).

Another significant question we need to ask ourselves as leaders of faith communities is this: How important is the community I lead in *shaping me* as a leader in deed as well as in word, title, or position? Remember the "lion" inside the marble!

The question reminds us of the relationship of clear vision and deep humility to the discipline of listening to others in the community we lead. Humility demands intense listening, which is so much more than allowing another to talk while waiting for a chance to respond.

Nouwen (1985) stated it powerfully: "The beauty of listening is that those who are listened to start feeling accepted, start taking their words more seriously.... Listening is a form of spiritual hospitality by which you invite strangers to become friends.... True listeners no longer have an inner need to make their presence known. They are free to receive, to welcome, to accept." (March 12 devotional)

We listen to what is said, and for what is not said. There is no need to prove ourselves by speeches, arguments, or interruptions. We observe body language. We listen for insights from brothers and sisters in Christ who help us revise a vision, plan, or program and make it better. Again, ownership of the vision must be "owned" by the group—individually and collectively—who are asked to embrace the vision and share in the implementation.

It may be meaningful to return to Chapter Two for a few minutes and read the scriptural passages and comments on Ephesians 4:25 (NIV): "Speak honestly; do not lie; Why? Because we are members of the body of Christ."

Collaboration is messy...but required! A few years ago, I had the privilege of speaking to a group of Church of the Nazarene educators in Johannesburg, South Africa. The setting was the first Consultation on Global Faculty Development for the denomination. Nazarene educators spent a week together probing the possibilities of an Academy for International Education.

My part in the conference program was to lead two sessions on the subject of institutional collaboration. The title of my presentation was "Institutional Collaboration as Academic Strategy." I addressed the need for intra-and inter-institutional strategy as foundational for the denomination to "maximize access" to the rich resources of the educational institutions of the Church of the Nazarene worldwide.

It was a wonderful experience for me. I met many friends from around the world. However, something happened to me while I was there. My purpose was to assist other educators. I found myself asking some hard questions about my self-management and leadership character at MVNU and the degree to which I modeled the robust community and intentional collaboration I *preached*. I questioned myself about my personal integrity. Was the strategic process I thought I was championing at MVNU falling on deaf ears? If so, why?

I returned to the university campus determined to share with the faculty and staff my "moment of truth," to outline some specific steps for us to take together and to request for the campus community to hold me accountable to my word. If trust is the foundation of effective leadership, then *I must be the change* I seek in the MVNU faculty and staff, before institutional collaboration is to become a way of life on our campus.

Let me summarize what I said to the educators in Johannesburg, and then identify some questions I, subsequently, asked the MVNU faculty and staff about our relationships. I suggested that every organization needs a "champion" for the collaborative process, if partnering or collaborating is to become a way of life for an institution and not just an intellectual game. I presented some lessons learned about collaboration.

1. Using collaboration to manage change is challenging.

2. A clear vision and felt need are required for success.

3. Regular communication is the glue of collaboration.

4. Active, committed leadership at the senior administrative level and an informed and broad-based steering committee are required.

5. The greater the trust and communication, the faster and more profound is the benefit.

6. Institutional collaboration must become institutional strategy.

Before I completed the presentation, I made some remarks using quotes I had included for them in a booklet distributed to the group. However, as I was speaking to

THEM, I found myself speaking to myself. I sincerely wanted to increase the level of involvement and trust between the administration and the campus community of employees. The power of three (or more) as affirmed in Ecclesiastes is a powerful image and necessary concept for an organization, institution, or church seeking to embrace robust community and intentional collaboration as strategy. Indeed, robust community and intentional collaboration must reflect themselves in implementation strategy. This is my passion and will only happen if we intensely believe with Helen Keller (as cited in Lash, 1980):

"Alone we can do so little, together we can do so much" (p. 489).

More specifically, I returned to MVNU and shared with the campus community eight "community-building" commitments to which I bound myself as I continued to lead the university. Included in the list of eight were the following two.

I want to affirm and value each of you as brothers and sisters in Christ who choose to work at MVNU as a vocational calling.

I will work closely with a task force specifically and with the campus community during the next eighteen months to streamline the administrative and decision making structures. The goal is to facilitate, not inhibit, you in accomplishing your vocational assignments and realizing your ministry goals at the university.

I shared with the campus community the proverb of the Kikuyu people of Africa:

"WHEN ELEPHANTS FIGHT, IT IS THE GRASS THAT SUFFERS."

The proverb means that when the people in power (the leaders) fight, it is the *grassroots* people who get hurt. I wanted to empower and support the faculty and staff, yet, wondered if the structure presently in place facilitated or inhibited the grassroots of the university from working and relating at their peak potential.

I concluded my remarks to the faculty and staff by stating, "In a new and profound way since my Johannesburg experience, I want to understand, embrace, and lead this academic faith community with *integrity, character, vulnerability, community, courage, conviction, gratitude, hope and trust.* These self-leadership convictions shape a leader who seeks to lead from a Christian value base. "

Did I succeed in all that was outlined to the university faculty and staff? No! Interestingly, more was accomplished than one might expect. The issue, however, is not so much a "checklist" of accomplishments as it is the growth of the leader in competence, character, and community building and the growth of the led!

After presenting this material to the faculty and staff, I continued to think about the broader theme of leadership character, particularly, as the imperative relates to leading a community of faith in the midst of diverse personalities, conflicting expectations, differing faith traditions, distinct assignments and various levels of maturity. Leadership character becomes the issue. Self-leadership precedes community-building leadership. Character counts!

Leadership character is the connection between "Robust Community" and institutional collaboration. For community building to be vibrant, and for intentional collaboration to be effective, a shared vision of leadership and the ministry of every believer must be shared, embraced, and celebrated.

The big community and collaborative question for ministry organizations, educational institutions, and local churches is this: How can this institution, ministry, or congregation mobilize its members and collaborate with supporters and members within and beyond the four walls of the organization's physical structure to equip *others* for *their* ministry—for worship, discipleship and disciple-making, outreach, and fellowship—in such a way that *they* will be prepared to teach others? (II Timothy 2:2)

Bennis and Biederman (1997) reminded us, "'*None of us is as smart as all of us'" (p. 1).* Mother Theresa is quoted as saying, "What you are doing I may not be able to do... What I am doing you may not be able to do...*but all of us together are doing something beautiful for God"* (Source unknown).

Let's talk more about the *method* of *intentional* collaboration within a faith community. Collaboration is a process through which parties see different aspects of a problem through the eyes of the Spirit of God and prayerfully and constructively explore their differences and search for solutions that go beyond their own limited vision of what is possible. They believe that followers of Christ have gifts, talents, abilities, insights, and contributions to make regarding the mandate for ministry.

Collaboration is all about individual relationships purposively working together to accomplish a shared outcome. It is a choice. It is difficult, messy, clumsy, and time-consuming; but it is the only way groups, institutions, and local churches can move from the routine and ordinary to impact and accomplishment.

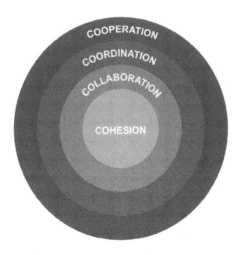

Figure 4.7. The collaborative journey. (Inspired by Winer, 1994)

Collaborative leaders do not act in isolation. "They are inclusive rather than exclusive in approach. They are willing to listen to and collaborate with those whose views and style may differ from their own" (Sofield & Kuhn, 1995, p. 38).

Positive change can occur when people with different perspectives are received and everyone is regarded as a peer. There must be a high level of involvement, a clear purpose, adequate resources, and the power to decide and implement. This mutually beneficial and well-defined "working together" relationship is entered into by two or more organizations to achieve common goals. The relationship includes a commitment to a jointly developed structure, with an authority and accountability understanding for success and for the sharing of resources and rewards.

The critical challenge for the collaborative leader relates to where people fit in the process, project, or initiative. We seek to take people and groups from where they are to where they want to go. Involving people in

136

different ways is the key. It is a means to an end, a way of life, rather than an end. To get to our destination "end points," individuals with common interests come together working for common solutions to common problems.

The key is to choose the right level of involvement, then increase intensity. The big issue is to get the right people in the right place doing the right thing. The *pay-off for collaboration* does not come easily or quickly. It is the long-term perspective that must be seen and kept in view. Winer (1994) compared the payoff for collaboration to the lily pond phenomenon (Figure 4.8).

Persons engaging in collaborative initiatives continually ask: What *value* can I contribute to the others? What value can they contribute to me? What can we do *together for the ministry and mission of an organization, the local church, or individual members* that could not be accomplished separately or solo?

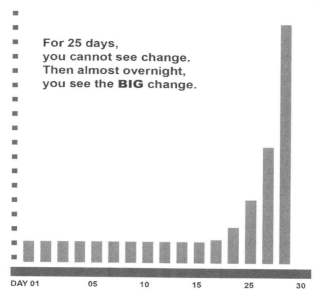

Figure 4.8. The lily pod phenomenon. (Inspired by Winer, 1994)

137

Not all contributions of members will be of equal value. Collaboration does not make everyone equal but has the potential of moving participating individuals and groups to a new level of ministry effectiveness. The benefit to community building and intentional collaboration is the overall lift and accomplishment of the group and the value members find in what they are doing. In successful collaboration, the *extraordinary* becomes the o r d i n a r y. Remember

"None of us is as smart as all of us"
(Bennis & Biederman, 1997, p. 1).

I remember Dr. Mike Winer (1994), an authority on institutional collaboration, speaking in a plenary session at Mount Vernon Nazarene University at the close of a three-year intense focus on intra- and inter-institutional collaboration. Among other quotes, he gave was this one from Barbara Cristy, "Leadership springs up at the *intersection* of personal passion and public needs."

The definition caught my attention for several reasons, particularly, because it addressed the issue of passion as it relates to churches or the institution(s) we serve. Winer said, "We often approach collaboration "intellectually," but with little passion. Our response to the passion of others must be, *Wow!!!*

I will not soon forget Winer's 1994 challenge: Do not confuse *information* and *inspiration*. Inspiration is the key. His challenge was clear. "Give 20% of effort to information; 80% of effort to inspiration."

The key characteristics of effective collaboration are mutual respect, understanding, trust, appropriate cross section of members, open and frequent communication, sufficient funds, skilled convener, members sharing in

138

process and outcome, and multiple levels of decision-making. Essential to effective collaboration in faith communities are *personal* benefits, in areas of personal growth toward ministry and mission effectiveness, and *community* benefits, a collective move forward that could not have happened without the combined group effort and contribution. Both benefit contributions should be recognized.

In collaborative initiatives, we need not only to sing from the same hymnal—but also from the *same page*. A mission and vision statement on each collaborative initiative is essential for any organization. This "results" statement is the glue that holds the collaborative project together. The statement must be *results* oriented—not *doing* oriented. Collaboration is a *process*, not an *end*.

The context of collaboration includes shared vision, consistent communication, project context, broad-based involvement, a results-orientation, measurable and definable outcomes, and evaluation. If you tell people what outcomes are expected, you have built in evaluation. It is important in a local church or a university to put the desired results (desired outcomes) of institutional life and work before the faculty and staff or congregation, before asking them to collaborate. The same is true in the context of a ministry organization.

Often mission and vision statements use too many words and cover too much territory for our responsibility group to grasp. In the lack of a WHY, more attention is given to the HOW (micro-managing). It is *imperative*, then, to be specific about what an institution or local congregation is all about.

Collaboratively shape mission, vision, and priority statements. Early in my assignment at Mount Vernon Nazarene University, I shared with the Board that four priorities would guide me in making decisions regarding the use of my time:

1. Spiritual leadership to the campus community— staff, faculty, senior administrators, students and beyond;

2. University-wide strategic thinking, planning, and implementation;

3. Christian leadership development regionally and worldwide; and

4. Major donor cultivation and gifting and endowment development for MVNU.

Developing theological, organizational, and personal mission and vision statements take time. If you have not already done so, block off some time, get away from the routine, and begin the process. Give yourself several months for the process to germinate and bear fruit. Share your draft statement with family, trusted friends, colleagues, pastor, teacher, mentor, or with your governing board for feedback. It is a transforming experience!

What are some major components to be included in *your* mission and vision statement?

Educational institutions focus on students in their mission and vision statements. Students are the heart of educational institutions. At Mount Vernon Nazarene

University, through a six-month process of collaboration, the faculty, staff, and administration recommended to the Board of Trustees this statement:

Mount Vernon Nazarene University:
An academic community of faith,
Shaping Christ-like leaders and disciples
For lifelong service and global impact.

For local churches, focus on *transformed lives* of the persons involved in disciple making and the ministry and mission opportunities in your *mission and vision statements*. The National Development Institute recommends that the focus in nonprofits organizations should be *donor*-based, not institution or organization-based.

To drill somewhat deeper, ask these questions:

1. What are we about as a Christian university, theological education institution, local congregation, or ministry organization?

2. How can the ministry we embrace intersect with the needs, interest, and goals of those we seek to lead and serve?

Start by clarifying the why of the ministry. Inspire your people with the big vision. Paint the picture big! Involve the aspirations, strengths, and skills, even legacy questions. Embody the values of the community you lead. Model the essence and message of the organization you serve.

Collaborative leaders, including local church pastors and institutional presidents or organization leaders, are passionate about fostering a *culture of collaboration* within their responsibility group to believe that they, collectively, and each person, individually, can make a difference in

141

this world. Enabling others to work together to make a difference is a high calling and phenomenally fulfilling experience! Work together in community to accomplish what no one person alone could achieve!

Back to the basic question. What is the mission and vision of "your" local church, ministry organization, or education institution? Can you identify the core or essence of your churches, organizations, or institutions around which your people are rallying? What is your faith community (as an organism and organization) about? What is the reason for assembling together on Sundays or at other times of the week?

Remember to get people involved at some level. And, continually listen to their *interests*, watch for *their* passion, listen to *their* stories even as you share with them *why* we do what we do. Passionate collaborative leaders must provide the framework.

Robust community building increases with a clear focus on the essence, the "why," the mission and vision of the local church, ministry organization, or educational institution...*and* the people around them! Leaders intentionally collaborate, *inspire and weave* the people *they serve* around a *cause, a purpose, a mission, a vision, and their own passion!*

Let your organizational or institutional vision statement be seen throughout the facility you use, the congregation, on your stationery, on posters and signs, on bulletin boards, and in the classrooms and offices. Be consistent. In providing consistency, the culture of a faith community and service organization will change.

Again, paint the vision of what we want the community to be (the kind of robust community you envision for the group). Connect the dots! Inspire! Define and embody the essence of the community. Listen! Listen, Listen! Write it on the "doorposts!" "Bleed" for a robust community and intentional collaboration for ministry and mission.

Involve, involve, involve the people we lead. Provide consistency in articulating our essence and identity. In so doing, prioritizing will become easy. Then you and I will know why and when to collaborate, for "what" purpose, and with whom!

1. Collaborative leaders need to do several things simultaneously.

2. Go slow and build success. (Do less…but with likelihood of success.

3. Capture individual passions. (Don't squash strong commitment.)

4. Decide what the "core" is. Other issues will follow.

5. Find multiple venues to communicate the mission and vision.

6. Listen and involve!

The motivation for a culture of collaboration is in the *essence* — the overarching vision. Let the *essence* drive the collaborative efforts. Trust is not the same as liking others, being liked, or getting my own way. Trust is about reliance and hope.

Reliance means that you do what you say you will do. Hope is trusting to achieve what we say we will achieve. "Trust is at the heart of fostering collaboration. It's 'the' central issue in human relationships within and outside the organization" (Kouzes & Posner, 1995, p. 163). There rarely can be too much communication in collaboration. Communicate! Communicate! Communicate!

"May the God who gives endurance and encouragement give you a spirit of unity among yourselves as you follow Christ Jesus, so that with one heart and mouth you may glorify the God and Father of our Lord Jesus Christ" (Romans 15:5).

"May they be brought to complete unity to let the world know that you sent me and have loved them even as you have loved me" (John 17:23).

"Make every effort to keep the unity of the Spirit through the bond of peace" (Ephesians 4:30).

"Now to each one the manifestation of the Spirit is given for the common good" (I Corinthians 12:7).

"Be completely humble and gentle; be patient, bearing with one another in love" (Ephesians 4:2).

The Significant Role of Encouragement

We conclude this chapter on METHODS by reminding ourselves of the importance of encouragement and support within the faith communities we lead. These "seven essentials" for encouraging others is adapted from the book, *Encouraging The Heart*, written by James Kouzes and Barry Posner (2003). The appendix to the book has 150 very specific strategies to encourage others as we work with them in community.

The First Essential: SET CLEAR STANDARDS
Communicate expectations clearly. Volunteers want and need clarity.

The Second Standard: EXPECT THE BEST
Affirm others often (watch your words). Seek to encourage, not discourage.

The Third Essential: PAY ATTENTION
Listen attentively. Seek first to understand. Lead always. Use words if necessary.

The Fourth Essential: PERSONALIZE RECOGNITION
Be specific in recognition, and compliment them often. Make it genuine.

The Fifth Essential: TELL THE STORY
Share *their* story (accomplishments, ministry, successes). *Their* story!

The Sixth Essential: CELEBRATE TOGETHER
Celebrate small (and large) victories often and with others. Look for opportunities to celebrate together!

The Seventh Essential: SET THE EXAMPLE
Lead the way. Set the Example. Do not expect of others what you would not do yourself. Model the mission. Be the change you desire to see in others (p. 45).

Develop your own list of *essentials* for encouraging others. If you are comfortable with the above list, then identify dates, events, persons, processes, accomplishments, to say privately and publicly, "Thank you," or "Congratulations," or "We are proud of you." Do it often. Spontaneous celebrations are fun as well as the more formal occasions. Have fun. Laugh and celebrate! Make it personal and make it corporate.

Don't overlook the first essential. Volunteers desire clear instructions for the tasks requested. Their time available to do what is requested is limited. When the assignment is completed, compliment them and find a way to celebrate! Lead the way in recognizing accomplishments. Others will follow you! Be known as one who goes around encouraging others.

In Chapter Four, METHOD, we looked closely at Mentoring, Board Governance, Strategic Questions, Missional Planning, Robust Community and Intentional Collaboration as key strategies by which we equip and enable those for whom we are responsible for effective ministry and mission at home and far away. We are captured by this vision of ministry *with* and ministry *by* the people we serve.

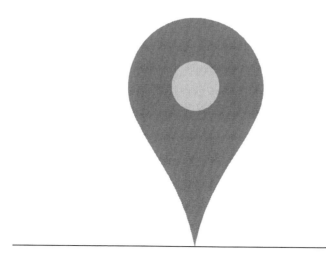

MARKER FIVE:

THE PAIN OF LEADING DECISIVELY IS EXPERIENCED IN THE TENSION BETWEEN GOOD AND GODLY PEOPLE... OVER VISION, VALUES AND TRADITIONS.

Chapter Five

MARKER FIVE:
THE PAIN OF LEADING DECISIVELY IS EXPERIENCED IN THE TENSION BETWEEN CONFLICTING VISION, VALUES, AND TRADITIONS.

Christian leaders believe that good and godly people can and do experience clear and intense differences.

Edward LeBron Fairbanks

The Joy and Pain of Leadership

I return often to a quote from Teddy Roosevelt, the 26th President of the United States, for encouragement, perspective, and comfort. Reflect again on these words:

> It is not the critic who counts, not the man who points out how the strong stumbles, or where the doer of deeds could have been better. The credit belongs to the man in the arena, whose face is marred by dust and sweat and blood; who strives valiantly...who spends himself in a worthy cause, who at the best knows in the end the triumph of high achievement, and at worst, if he fails, at least fails while daring greatly, so that his place shall never be with those cold and timid souls who have never known neither victory or defeat. (Roosevelt as cited in Brown, 2012, p. 1).

Sometimes, the visionary leaders experience the "pain of leadership" when a vision of the future is not accepted or grasped by those for whom the leader is responsible — individuals, it seems, to the leader, who often prefer the status quo. Much prayer and the Spirit of God empowering the leader will give the visionary courage, strength, and comfort as s/he guides a congregation and a ministry group through necessary (and sometimes painful) transitions.

In mentoring and teaching emerging leaders, we often focus on the joy of leadership (Figure 5.1) and not the pain in leadership (Figure 5.2). It is true that individuals in leadership positions have the potential to influence change and impact people, which is rewarding and energizes us. When a vision captures us, growth and expansion result. Surely, everyone will agree, this is right! We will move ahead. And we are grateful!

Figure 5.1. The joy of leadership. © E.L Fairbanks

Believing the action to take, policy to adopt, direction to pursue, or goal to adopt is God-given, the individual holds tenaciously to the vision for the assignment.

However, from the other extended arm is a hand firmly holding to reality — the *situation* or context in which the individual works or the *circumstances* (finances or facilities), which seem to dictate what can and cannot be done, or the *people* or followers who must embrace the vision if what is dreamed is to move from vision to action (Figure 5.2).

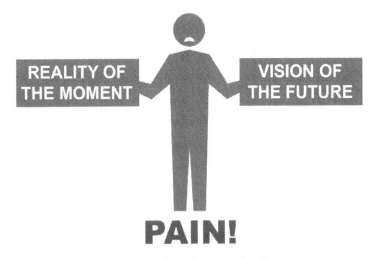

Figure 5.2. The pain of leadership. © E.L Fairbanks

We are stunned when those with whom we work reject the vision that is cast or challenge the vision that is presented. The tension in holding on to our vision and to the reality of the present situation often produces pain (see figure 5.2).

If we relax one arm and let go of the vision, we drift along with no direction (Figure 5.3).

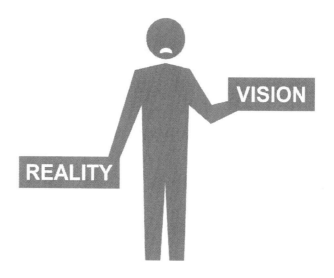

Figure 5.3. The temptation in leadership. © E.L Fairbanks

It is in holding, *intentionally*, to both vision and reality that the possibility exists for leaders to move from vision to action, and with this intentionality come both joy and pain for the leader.

Why? Sooner rather than later, Christian leaders are jolted when we experience this reality: Good and godly people often differ on how to reach mutually desired goals; and sometimes, these good and godly people COLLIDE. When the faith community is divided, the kingdom of God suffers and Satan laughs. This is the **pain** in leadership— intense pain!

I have come to see that these collisions occur, not necessarily because of good or bad ideas, noble or sinful goals, or right or wrong solutions. Rather, good and godly people most often collide over VISION, VALUES, and TRADITIONS in the faith community. We are caught in the middle of a divided group over where we should be going (vision), how we are going to get there (values), and

151

the way we have done it before (traditions).

*In the midst of these conflicting situations
and irreconcilable expectations placed on us,
what does it mean, really mean, to lead a divided
faith community with the mind of Christ?*

Managing Tensions and Transitions: Seven Anchors

There are at least seven essentials in managing the tension and transitions within a faith community as the leader guides the community from a vision to action to missional results. Seven "anchors" to hold us steady as faithful Christian leaders, as we grasp firmly to our vision and, at the same time, seek to move the church, university, region, or denomination to action.

Anchor #1: "Speak gracefully." Watch the words we speak. Words we speak can bless or "destroy" people. *"For out of the overflow of the heart the mouth speaks,"* so Jesus states in the Gospels (Matthew 12:34). As leaders we either encourage or discourage those with whom we work, uplift or diminish them, speak positively or negatively about them, or reflect cultural sensitivity or cultural "blindness" to them. We either focus on the other person or on ourselves.

I often ask myself this question. How do others feel when they leave my presence? Stronger or weaker? Larger or smaller about themselves? Confident or "scared"? Understood or misunderstood? Affirmed or manipulated? Blessed or "destroyed"?

Henri Nouwen (1991) quoted Arsenius, the Roman educator who exchanged his status and wealth for the solitude of the Egyptian desert, who said, "I have often repented of having spoken, but never of having remained silent" (p. 43).

According to Ephesians 4:25, God uses the words we speak to others within the Body of Christ to extend His grace through us to them! What a powerful and probing thought! Remember, the words we speak to those with whom we work, especially those who differ and even collide with us, can bless them or destroy them. Choose to bless them!

Anchor #2: "Live gratefully." Comparison is the root of inferiority. Do not "pout," cry, or complain. Be grateful. Comparison is so pervasive in our society — in the workforce, the family, the local church, or region, in our communities, and, particularly, within us. We can feel good about ourselves — our gifts, talents, and abilities — until we compare ourselves with the gifts, talents, and abilities of *other* people. We can believe our co-workers are adequate for the jobs we give to them until we compare their work — creativity, innovation, energy, and collegiality — with others.

Comparison destroys us within and robs us of joy, relationships, confidence, and peace. In the process, comparison saps our energy and drains us of enthusiasm. Comparison can transform us from being a delightful *boss*, supervisor, or pastor into a preoccupied, dejected, negative, and disgruntled individual that other people only endure.

What is the antidote to comparison? Three profound biblical qualities:

- *Gratitude!*
- *Thankfulness!*
- *Appreciation!*

153

We can choose to accept the people and provisions God in His wisdom has given to us. We can choose to work to bring out the best in others through seeing the best in them. In every situation, we can choose to be grateful, believing that God is in the midst of all that we are doing (I Thessalonians 5:18). Gratitude is the "life-giving" antidote to the negative impact of comparison.

Don't whine over what you do not have; be grateful—in all things—for what God has provided. Cultivate the discipline and practice of gratitude.

Not that I hold to this "anchor" in all situations today; but the more mature I become in my faith, the more I practice gratitude as a way of life. I usually sign my letters with the salutation, "Gratefully." This could be just routine and meaningless; but, for me, it is a constant remainder of the mindset I desire to cultivate in all situations.

A recently retired Old Testament scholar and I graduated from Nazarene Theological Seminary the same year and were both accepted into a well-known institution in the Northeastern United States. We both entered the graduate school at another master's degree level, believing that we would then move onto the doctoral program of the institution. To our shock, when we were nearing the completion of the academic program into which we had enrolled, both of us were informed that our applications for admission to the doctoral programs to which we had applied were denied! We were stunned. Embarrassed. Angry. Disappointed. Later, we found out that the faculty were in the process of reviewing and revising the doctoral programs; so all applications were frozen for the year in which we applied.

Both of us took pastorates upon completion of the Master of Theology degrees from this institution. What a blessing! Within several years, we both applied to other schools, continued pastoring, shifted our doctoral study focus, and, subsequently, completed our programs.

Although I did not understand it at the time, the "rejection" turned out to be a blessing in disguise for my wife and me. We enjoyed immensely our pastoral assignments and, as a result, I broadened the focus of my doctoral studies into areas beyond that which was originally planned. I soon began to seen the wisdom of the Lord in this process and acknowledged the new direction in our lives. My wife and I were fulfilled in our pastoral ministry, as we have been in our ministry in higher education since 1978!

Anchor #3: "Listen intently." Seek first to understand. Understanding, not agreement is the key to conflict management. "Good and godly" people *can* have honest and intense differences. After 30+ years in higher education administration, I affirm with confidence that *good and godly people not only differ but sometimes collide over vision and values.* And you have similar testimonies!

This is why I have come to see that *theological* vision (what I believe about people/what I *see* in them) precedes *organizational* vision (what I want for the organization, church, university, region, or denomination). I continue to pray often, "God, give me *your* eyes to really *see* the people with whom I live and work.

Humility demands intense listening by the person who leads others. Nouwen (1985a) statement is worth repeating: "The beauty of listening is that those who are listened to start feeling accepted, start taking their words more seriously.... Listening is a form of spiritual *hospitality* by

155

which you invite strangers to become friends..." (March 11 Devotional).

Edwin Friedman (2007) believed that the most important attribute of a leader is not knowledge or technique but what the leader brings in his/her presence. And the presence he/she needs is a "non-anxious" presence (p. 110).

According to Stone and Heen, (2014), listening is the first of four skills a leader needs to "navigate the body of the conversations" (p. 233). For Stone and Heen, listening includes "asking clarifying questions, paraphrasing the giver's view, and acknowledging their feelings" (p. 233).

Anchor #4: "Forgive freely." Be proactive in extending forgiveness. A spirit of forgiveness transforms and empowers leaders. One of my profound life lessons is this: Forgiveness has little to do with the external environment around me and everything to do with my "internal" condition! Extending forgiveness does not wait for the "other" to request forgiveness. Jesus on the cross said, "Father, forgive them, they know not what they do" (Luke 23:34).

Was Jesus naive? Did he really believe that those who were killing him did not know what they were doing? No! Did Jesus believe that by extending forgiveness, those who were slandering him and hurting him would cease their activity? No!

Jesus, in essence, was not going to permit what others **said** against Him or the evil they **did** against Him to create bitterness or resentment *within* Him and, thereby, create a rupture on the relationship with God His Father. It simply was not worth it! "Father, forgive them, they know not what they do" (Luke 23:34).

Extending forgiveness frees me from bondage to the other person. Too often, we permit persons who have offended us to control us. "Great leaders," we are told, "are shaped in the most challenging and difficult times." A spirit of forgiveness transforms and empowers leaders.

Anchor # 5: "Lead decisively." Combine clear vision, deep humility with intense resolve. We seldom "enjoy" the luxury of having all the information we need before making necessary decisions. Perhaps, you have heard it said, "One person's dream is another person's nightmare!" Yet, it is in this context that we live, work, and lead. It is in the tension between our *vision* for the future and the *reality* of the present that our decision making as leaders most often takes place.

As leaders, we constantly move between t w o needs: the need for long range and strategic planning for our assignments and the daily routine of budgets, personnel, facility management, and interpersonal conflicts. Sometimes, this balancing act is between macro managing (strategy focused on the big picture) and micro managing (staying focused on the small implementation details of our assignments).

I have often told the people with whom I work that I want to be a leader of faith and vision. But I do not want to cross the line to be an irresponsible leader, one whose actions defy rationality and reject the collective judgment of wise and mature saints. Yet, who determines where the "line" really is between *faith* and *irresponsibility?*

It is painful to have to choose between biblical imperatives (i.e., "go ye...and make disciples") and people needs (i.e. salary increases, equipment needs, and travel expenses). But sometimes, I made those decisions and so, perhaps, have you.

157

By now, you have heard me speak of the critical importance of RESPECT for those with whom we labor as we pursue the biblical mandate for mission and ministry. You have heard me discuss "respect" for our co-workers through the words we speak, expressing gratitude for them, listening to them intently, and forgiving freely.

In fact, respecting those with whom we differ — even collide with — is at the heart of what it means to *lead* with the Mind of Christ. However, at some point in our leadership roles, decisions have to be made. As I say this, we must remember that the real issue is not, "Must a decision be made?" Rather the question is, "*How*, within the community, are the decisions made and implemented?"

Especially in times of conflict over vision, decisions will need to be made — even when continuing differences exist! And, in these times, we will lead — and lead decisively — but from our knees and often with tears in our eyes! We must avoid *paralysis* — waiting until everyone agrees with us — when decisions need and must be made. Sometimes, perhaps often, we must move ahead without everyone within the community agreeing with the vision or direction to be taken. How do we move ahead, decisively, in these painful situations while, at the same time, showing Christian *respect* to those who differ with us?

We move ahead — decisively — through *prayer*, with them, for them, and for ourselves as leader. We move ahead through *collaboration*, involving them when and where we can in the process. We move ahead through the practice of *gratitude*, thanking God, and "them" for their gifts, talents, abilities, *and* testimony of faith. Pray alone. Pray together. Pray often. We pray for gentleness, kindness, compassion, patience, and love — even as we move ahead when a majority has spoken. We desire consensus, but some may differ and collide with you over the decision of the majority. Painful? Yes.

In this spirit of humility and brokenness, we move ahead confidently — believing that God is working in the midst of the difficult situation. In this spirit, we move ahead decisively, not with paralysis or uncertainty, but in kindness and compassion. Our actions are marked with the conviction that God has spoken His word of vision and direction, and that He will continue to lead His people to action even though the circumstances or attitudes may not give evidence of His work at the present time. This is leading with the mind of Christ — leading decisively in the midst of complex and difficult situations.

To lead decisively with Christian humility demands that we continue to nurture and develop skills in listening and communicating, timing and processing, affirming and encouraging, asking and inquiring, "gift" discernment and delegation, and, perhaps, other skills!

The more I understand about leading with the Mind of Christ, the more I realize how much I do not know. I am a committed lifelong learner and student of what is involved in leading decisively with clear vision, deep humility, and intense resolve.

Anchor #6: "Love deeply." Value people — not power or position. The evidence of leadership is seen in the lives of the followers. As leaders, you and I must keep remembering the many values we have in common with our colleagues. Focus on the matters that unite us, not divide us.

Over the years, I have tried to remember to trust my best moments when making decisions regarding employees. "Let your gentleness be known to all" (Philippians 4:4-7).

As leaders we must be passionate about communicating our personal, professional, and organizational vision, mission, and values to those with whom we work or for whom we are responsible. Lead the way and encourage others, for whom you are responsible, to memorize the strategic vision of the faith community you lead. Talk often about the "overarching priorities of our group." Collectively focus on the core values.

This is the bottom line: Try to enlarge the vision of the people about the work they are doing. Remember to paint the picture big! Assist them in discovering how they, in their particular assignments and with their specific gifts, fit into the grand scheme and purpose of the institution, organization, or church.

I wanted faculty, staff, and students to feel positive about working at MVNU and to believe that their assignment at the university was growth producing--personally and professionally. Value people and progress, not power and position.

Anchor #7: "Pray earnestly." Some issues are only resolved through intense prayer. Become the change you desire to see in others.

Caring leaders know that we do not have the power to change others. Change can take place, however, within *us*! In the midst of experiencing honest and intense differences between good and godly people, the "pray-er" can be changed and transformed!

160

Conflict situations can *produce* growth. They can also *inhibit* growth in the lives of leaders. Before God in prayer, we seek answers from Him to the two questions asked earlier: *What can I learn? How can I change?* In so asking, and seeking God's answers to these two questions for our lives as leaders, we *are* changed! Increasingly, by God's grace, *we* become the change we desire to see in *others*, who may or may not be impacted by what happens within us. But, what happens to us is transformative! We grow. We change. We mature. We increasingly exemplify the change we desire to see in others! And, in the process, we experience the peace of God, which transcends understanding. We are "freed" from insisting on change within others. Through earnest prayer, caring leaders ask the right questions, and trust God with the results...even as we are changed in the process!

Qualities That Characterize and Convict Me

These qualities convict me at my worst and characterize me at my best. The "anchors" hold me steady as I seek to move the group for which I am responsible from vision to action to results, especially when good and godly people collide over vision, values, and traditions. In summary:

1. I want my words to be *grace-giving*, life-generating and inspiring to others and not discouraging, depressing, and draining utterances.

2. I want to be known as a person who is forever *grateful*, regardless of the situation, believing that God is in the midst of everything I do and is working to bring good in every situation.

3. I want to *listen* to and respect the people with whom I work, to understand them — and for them to understand me — even if we do not agree with each other. I want to initiate *forgiveness* when I have been offended, because I don't have the energy or strength to carry the heavy burden and guilt of an unforgiving spirit.

4. I want to *lead decisively* with clear vision, deep humility, and intense resolve, even as I experience the pain of holding tenaciously to the vision while acknowledging the realities of my situation.

5. I want my relationship with others to *energize* them; to have a positive impact on their lives; and to enable them, in some small way, to grow and become stronger in their faith, their confidence in themselves, and their competence at work, as a result of their interaction with me as their leader.

6. I want *change* to be seen in me, even as I desire to see change in others.

Jim Collins (2001), in his book, *Good to Great,* talks about the critical characteristics of the leaders. He speaks of humility and fierce resolve as essential for Level 5 or top leaders. I believe that whatever else you discover in decisive, servant leaders you will find that they:

1. **Speak gracefully.** They watch the words they speak.

2. **Live gratefully.** They don't "cry;" they are grateful.

3. **Listen intently.** They seek first to understand.

4. **Forgive freely.** They are proactive in extending forgiveness.

5. **Lead decisively.** They avoid paralysis in decision-making with humility.

6. **Love deeply.** They value people, not power.

7. **Pray earnestly.** They embrace change in themselves even as desire it in others.

Which one of these "anchors" do you need most in your present leadership assignment?

_____

As you experience the tension between the vision God has given you and the reality of your present situation, in which of these areas do you _most_ need God to hold you steady?

_____

As you move from vision to action to results, perhaps, in the midst of differences and collisions, what is your greatest need?

_____

One more question. Which of these seven anchors represent your greatest strength? Be specific. Be personal.

Be honest. It's vitally important for us to affirm our strength, even as we acknowledge our need. Build on your strength. Work on your greatest weakness so that it becomes your strength.

The Elusiveness of Contentment (in the Midst of Pain)

When conflicts and collisions occur within the fellowship, the temptation will be to give up and perhaps move on. On several occasions, I have even engaged in "pity parties," where I complained to God. In one of these "feeling sorry for myself" times, I began to reflect on the elusiveness of contentment. What does it mean to be content? And what is the nature of contentment

Does it mean that Christians must be passive and accept as their duty to God and individuals whatever pain that comes their way? Is contentment the same as resignation? Does biblical contentment imply a lack of ambition, desire for advancement, or vision of increased leadership responsibilities in a new or old work assignment?

The Apostle Paul in Philippians 4:11-13 speaks of the gift of contentment: *"I have learned to be content whatever the circumstances. I know what it is to be in need, and I know what it is to have plenty. I have learned the secret of being content in any and every situation, whether well fed or hungry, whether living in plenty or want. I can do everything through him who gives me strength."*

Especially in the tension of holding tenaciously to a God-given vision, while at the same time, grasping firmly to the reality of the present situation, biblical contentment is elusive. Contentment as described by Paul emerges as pivotal and transformative. It holds us steady when we are tempted to run or simply walk away. Biblical contentment is elusive because of (a) the irony of contentment; (b) the barriers to contentment; and (c) the secret of contentment. In painful situations for the leader within a faith community, especially, when we are upset with everyone else, Paul's guidance on contentment is particularly insightful to leaders.

164

The irony of contentment. The irony is this: We tend to think that we know what is best for our lives and our leadership assignments, and we ask God to agree (and if God grants our prayers, we will be content)! The text reminds us that God can give us inward peace in *whatever* situation He places us! Paul wrote these words on contentment while in prison. The previous two years he had been in another prison near Jerusalem, insulted by the Roman governor of the area, shipwrecked on his way to Rome, without food for 14 days, and then placed under house arrest when he arrived in Rome! And these seemingly disastrous experiences follow his great teaching and preaching and his three missionary journeys as recorded in the book of Acts. But did Paul moan? Complain? Whine? Blame others for his predicament? Engage in a "pity party"?

This is fascinating. In Rome, while in prison, he did not focus on what he could do if he had more resources, were in another location, if he worked for a different boss, or had Christian co-workers. He did not focus on "Why?" "Why me?" or "What if?" Instead, while in chains in Rome, Paul wrote what we know as the Prison Epistles: Philippians, Ephesians, Colossians, and Philemon! He "bloomed" where he was planted! According to Philippians 4:7, God gave Paul contentment and an inner peace. It is amazingly ironic how tomorrow takes care of itself, when we give our best to the workplace and ministry God has given to us today.

You may not work at the place you prefer, earn the money you desire, have the governing board you desire, or the parishioners you believe you need, or the major gifts you need to accomplish the big projects in your ministry. In these very situations, ironically, as difficult, unfair, and challenging as they may seem and be, you can experience a contentment that defies understanding.

Biblical contentment is elusive because of the *irony* of contentment. God's ways are not *our* ways. Paul starts at a different point: "I know what it means to be in need…or to have plenty; to be well fed or hungry. And he challenges us to do the same and to affirm the appropriate parallels in our lives.

A barrier to contentment is our *circumstances*. Paul could have said, "Why am I in prison? Why didn't I listen to friends?" (His friends in the cities of Tyre and Caesarea begged Paul not to continue his journey to Jerusalem knowing that he would face persecution and prison.) You and I have these continual temptations:

> "If I had just listened to…"
> "Life is greener on the other side."
> "If I were there, I could… "
> "If I had this… or that…"

Paul's response to his friends who begged him not to continue to Jerusalem (Acts 21:14) was clear: *"I will do God's will."* Paul proceeded to Jerusalem and he was at peace.

Another barrier to contentment is *people*. In my 30 plus years of higher education administration, I have come to see that in any situation, there will be problems and possibilities when people are involved. Will we focus on the problems? Or will we focus on the possibilities and potentials?

In Paul's situation, he witnessed to many in *jail*! He wrote letters to the young churches at Philippi, Ephesus, Colossae, and to Philemon. Paul encourages us to focus on the *possibilities* of our circumstances and not exclusively or morbidly on our problems with the people with whom we live, worship, and work.

166

Biblical contentment is elusive because of the *irony* of contentment and the *barriers* to contentment. Paul guides us also to:

The secret of contentment. The secret of contentment is not grounded in the people who disappoint us, circumstances that distract us, or problems that overwhelm us. The secret of biblical contentment is grounded in gratitude.

Contentment is rooted in a *focus* on God and *His* mercy and grace, not in a *preoccupation* with people and problems. The *foremost quality* of a *contented* person is **gratefulness**.

Listen again to Philippians 4:5-6. *"Let your gentleness be evident to all. Do not be anxious about anything, but in everything, by prayer and petition, with thanksgiving, present your request to God."* And what is the result? Paul tells us: *"And the peace of God which transcends all understanding will guard your hearts and minds in Christ Jesus!"*

Gratitude – thanksgiving – arises out of our acceptance that *all* of life is grace – as an undeserved and unearned gift – a grace gift – from the Father's hand.

This theocentric or God-centered character of gratitude is anchored in *ruthless trust* in *God* who is *sovereign* and whose *providential care* guides His People.

I am slowly coming to see, very slowly, that contentment does not make us *grateful*. Rather it is *gratitude* that makes us *contented*. When things go wrong, when people disappoint us, when our colleagues do not understand us, and when it appears that irreconcilable differences exist within the faith community between good and godly people, we can *choose* to *believe* in the sovereignty of God. In the midst of inner unrest, we can

167

choose to believe in His watchful care over our lives in the midst of doubts, questions, conflicts, and persecution.

In these sometimes humanly miserable situations, we can choose to believe that:

> In His time,
> In His time,
> He makes all things beautiful,
> In His time.
> Lord, please show me everyday
> As your teaching me your way,
> that you do just what you say,
> In *your* time!
> (Bible, *Sing to the Lord*, #575).

Often, this is a convictional affirmation, based alone in radical trust in a Sovereign God. When emotions and circumstances do not suggest this affirmation of faith, we can choose to believe in the Holy God of Grace and Mercy to see us through.

We often quote by memory Paul's great statement in Philippians 4:13: *"I can do all things through Christ who gives me strength."* It is a great verse to remind us to be strong and take courage because our faith is in Christ...not ourselves or others. Paul gives this great verse to us in the context of his discussion of contentment:

> I can do *all* things, whether in need and hungry,
> or with plenty and well fed.
> **In either set of circumstances —**
> I can do *everything* God wants me to do
> *through Christ* who gives me strength.

Whatever the circumstance or conditions, and regardless of the people — their attitudes and their treatment of us, be grateful for the Christ who dwells within you and me and gives us contentment in the midst of these difficult situations and circumstances. Be grateful — thankful — that, in the midst of stress, pressure, and, perhaps, misunderstanding, God is teaching *us* things about ourselves, others, life, faith, and trust that we would not — *could not* — *have* learned **without** these experiences!

Contentment is grounded in a heart filled with gratitude. Even in prison, the Triune God was still in control of Paul's life. Gratitude, for Paul, was not conditioned in good circumstances, understanding employees, pleasant co-workers, or that great salary. Rather his gratitude was rooted in a ruthless TRUST in the Sovereign God of Grace and Mercy.

Paul challenges us to "give thanks with a grateful heart," and he teaches us that gratitude is not grounded in murmuring, grumbling, faultfinding, or complaining. Rather the secret of contentment — for Paul, and for us — is in the conviction that God is *big* enough to handle *any* situation we encounter.

Pain and Christian Hope in Confusing Times

Napoleon Bonaparte is reported to have said, "Leaders are dealers in hope." For the Christian leader, this is especially true in situations within a faith community when good and godly people have clear and distinct differences over vision and values.

Months before the 2001-02 school year began, I was scheduled to speak on September 12, 2001, to MVNU students in a chapel service. The events of September 11 shook us to the core on campus, as it did to many around the world. I will never forget praying with students, staff, faculty, and their families as they came to the MVNU R.R. Hodges Chapel/Auditorium throughout the afternoon of September 11. At 6:00 p.m., the chaplain and his staff led the campus community in a meaningful service of prayer and reflection.

My sermon theme for the Wednesday morning, September 12, chapel service changed radically. With much prayer and not much sleep, I spoke to our campus family on the subject, "Why Do Good People Suffer?" The text for the sermon was the Old Testament book of Habakkuk. All of us, it seemed, were asking questions and seeking answers regarding the problem of evil and human suffering.

Habakkuk, you may remember, was an Old Testament prophet who was deeply distressed by the apparent injustice that prevailed in the world. He attempted to reconcile the evil of his day to the goodness and the righteous character of God.

As a prophet of God, he was concerned with the suffering of his people.

Were they not the chosen of God? Why would God use a heathen nation to chastise His own people?

Habakkuk reminded God that they were not as bad as the Chaldeans whom God was using to humiliate or chasten Judah, the children of God. In the midst of Habakkuk's complaining to God, (in Chapter 1), he affirms boldly: "The just shall live by his faith" (Habakkuk 2:4).

When God told Habakkuk that Babylon would conquer Israel, the prophet felt that this was not just. Without hesitation, he asks God why He would allow a heathen and cruel nation to oppress *His* people? Habakkuk

170

concludes his power-packed, three-chapter book not only with the great affirmation that "the just shall live by his faith" but with these words near the close of Chapter 3:

> *"Though the fig tree does not bud and*
> *there are no grapes on the vines,*
> *Though the olive crops fail and*
> *the fields produce no food,*
> *Though there are no sheep in the pen and*
> *no cattle in the stalls,*
> *Yet, I will rejoice in the Lord,*
> *I will be joyful in God my Savior."*
> Habakkuk 3:17-19

Fairbanks' paraphrase of these verses:
When God appears silent, when there is no apparent evidence that God hears or even understands the situation, when all that I have worked for seems lost. In these moments, we choose to believe radically in a God who is faithful and true; We stake our lives on His promise to never leave us nor forsake us; and we pray, "We don't know what to do, but we are looking to you."

Our faith, in these moments, is not based on *feeling* but on the *conviction* that God is sovereign and will bring good out of every situation in which we find ourselves. God dealt with Habakkuk patiently until he could see that Babylon was being used by God to discipline Israel and that Babylon itself would also face the judgment of God.

The providence of God does not mean that disappointment and trouble will not come. It does mean that nothing, not even the greatest tragedy, the bitterest persecution, the worst misfortune, or death of the body can do any permanent harm or separate us from the Love of God!

Anne and I celebrated our 40th wedding anniversary in June 2002 on a summer weekend in New York City. Each day we were in the Big Apple, we walked around

"Ground Zero." The huge number of pictures, cards, tributes, and letters overwhelmed us. Written prayers were attached to anything and everything around the perimeter. We paused and read many of the tributes, letters, cards, and prayers.

In the midst of such grief and tragedy, I found myself singing over and over again the chorus of the old hymn:

On Christ, the solid Rock, I stand;
All other ground is sinking sand.
All other ground is sinking sand.

Verse two of the song, written in 1834, seemed especially appropriate on this occasion in 2002:

When darkness seems to hide His face,
I rest on His unchanging grace.
In every high and stormy gale,
My anchor holds within the veil.
(Bible, 1993, p. 436)

As Christians, our hope is in Christ! By grace alone, with conviction we affirm this hope in the midst of the suffering from economic deprivation, vast social disparity, political dictatorship, or the hideous work of terrorists.

Our hope as Christians is in the God of Abraham, Isaac, and Jacob, the God who was in Christ reconciling the world unto Himself. **The center of the Christian gospel is the reconciliation of all creation to God through Jesus Christ.** The old gospel song has it right, "This world is not my home, I'm just 'apassing' through." We are to live in the world but not be of the world

As Christians, our hope is not for this life only, it is for life eternal with the Triune God. The question we face as followers of Jesus Christ is: Are we living faithfully as members of the "community of the King," with Kingdom "eyes," ruthless trust, and a radical hope?

Anne, Stephen, and I lived in Manila, Philippines, prior to moving in 1989 to Mount Vernon, Ohio. At the time, the average per capital income was $700 a year. We worshipped with beautiful Filipino Christians, whose joy was contagious. Their church facilities were simple. Their homes were modest and meager. Many traveled to the market each day for food because of no refrigeration in their homes.

Yet, these Christians were joyful because their hope was not in their government, their job, or their income. Their hope was in Jesus Christ for their *salvation* and for their *comfort*. They truly believed that, "This world is not my home, I'm just 'apassing' through."

Hope in Christ does not mean we will avoid or be able to ignore suffering. We know that hope born of faith is nurtured and purified through pain, suffering, and difficulty. The basis of our hope, however, has to do with the One who is stronger than the suffering we encounter.

The people of Israel repeatedly reflected on their history and discerned God's guiding hand in the many painful events. Memory reminds us of the faithfulness of God in the hard times and in the joyful moments. Without memory, there is no expectation.

With expectation, we experience the minutes, hours, and days of our life differently. Christian hope is not dependent on peace in the land or justice in the world.

A chorus we sang often in MVNU chapel services includes these words:

My life is in You, Lord,
My strength is in You, Lord,
My hope is in You, Lord,
In You, it's in You.

I will praise You with all of my life,
I will praise You with all of my strength,
With all of my life,
With all of my strength,
All of my hope is in You!

My life is in You, Lord,
My strength is in You, Lord,
My hope is in You, Lord,
In You, it's in You.
(author unknown)

Hope is willing to leave some questions unanswered. Hope makes you see God's guiding hand not only in the gentle and pleasant moments but also in the shadows of disappointment and darkness.

Why? Because we believe! In a memorial chapel service at MVNU on September 11, 2002, we sang this chorus:

BECAUSE WE BELIEVE

We believe in God the Father,
We believe in Christ, the Son,
We believe in the Holy Spirit,
We are the church and we stand as one.

We believe in the Holy Bible,
We believe in the virgin birth,
We believe in the resurrection,
That Christ one day will return to earth.

We believe in the blood of Jesus,
We believe in eternal life,
We believe in His blood that frees us,
To become the Bride of Christ.

(Chorus)
Holy, holy, holy is our God,
Worthy, worthy, worthy is our King!
All glory and honor are His to receive,
To Jesus we sing because we believe!
(lyrics by Don Moen, 1997)

May these words speak grace, peace and hope to us as we reflect upon the leadership "hope" of reconciliation and transformation — individually and collectively — especially in difficult and confusing times!

Leaders are dealers in hope. Servant leaders radiate Christian hope in confusing and conflicting times in a community of faith.

We do not often talk about the pain of leadership; but it is real, nevertheless. Good and godly people experience clear and intense differences. And we are called to faithfully serve in the midst of these conflicts, even when the differences between visions and values appear irreconcilable.

Habakkuk and Paul provide words of guidance for us. Be content. Live by your faith. *"Let your gentleness be known to all"* (Philippians 4:5).

You may experience situations where leaders have been "too content" and are very happy with the status quo. Family, friends, or a governing board may need to return to the "seven anchors" in the midst of confronting with care.

Give thanks with a grateful heart and radiate hope...even in the painful times! Gratitude is the difference between changing a situation with frustration or without frustration. Gratitude!

MARKER SIX:

THE EVIDENCE OF LEADING DECISIVELY IS REFLECTED IN THE QUALITATIVE GROWTH OF THE LED.

Chapter Six

MARKER SIX:
THE EVIDENCE OF LEADING DECISIVELY IS REFLECTED IN THE QUALITATIVE GROWTH OF THE LED.

Leadership is known by the personalities it enriches, not by those it dominates or captivates. Leadership is not a process of exploitation of others for extraneous ends. It is a process of helping others to discover themselves in the achieving of aims that have become intrinsic to them. The proof of leading is in the qualitative growth of the led as individuals and as group members.

Harold W. Reed

The Servant Leader Is Servant First

The servant leader is a servant first.... It begins with the natural feeling that one wants to serve, to serve first. Then conscious choice brings one to aspire to lead. The difference manifests itself in the care taken by the servant — first to make sure that other people's highest priority needs are being served. The best test, and difficult to administer, is: do those served grow as persons; do they, while being served, become healthier, wiser, freer, more autonomous, more likely themselves to become servants? And, what is the effect on the least privileged in society; will they benefit, or at least not be further deprived? (Greenleaf, 1977, pp. 13-14.)

This chapter explores the rich relationship between the leader and the led. Since the leader's goal is to nurture the led, we will examine six qualities (trust, brokenness, gratefulness, hospitality, compassion, and endurance) that will assist the leader in pursuing her/his vocational mission of leading, leading decisively, with a vision to serve.

Stated differently, what values, goals, and attitudes are necessary for a leader to bring out the best and nurture effectively those being served, so that they are equipped to grow as persons more likely themselves to become servants and servant leaders? With what tools and characteristics should the leader come prepared to accomplish the task of leading decisively while serving? How can an individual lead in such a way that the persons served grow in the process, as the leader and the led work together to accomplish agreed upon goals for the advancement of the Kingdom? Bringing out the best and nurturing growth in those we lead are evidences of Christian leadership.

This chapter harkens back to MARKER TWO. In Chapter Two, we explored how the leader is a conduit of God's power, how the servant leader's power comes from God, and how humility with the led is the overall character the Christian servant leader should employ to be effective. In this chapter on *evidence*, we will go into detail on the qualities of the effective, servant leader and qualities the leader needs to internalize to be effective.

The six core qualities (Figure 6.1) are the servant leader's foundation for leading decisively. Employing these six core qualities will lead to the qualitative growth of the led or the "Evidence" of effective servant, visionary, and decisive leadership. In the following six sections, we will explore how decisive leaders have employed each of the six qualities. These represent the leader's *toolkit* for successful servant leadership.

Be the change we seek to produce in others.

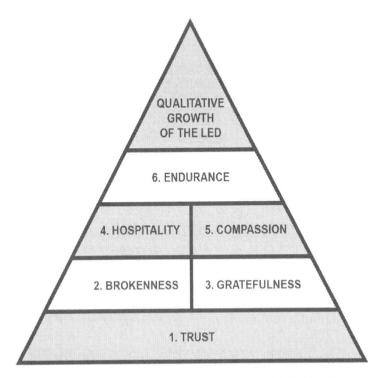

Figure 6.1. Core qualities of a servant leader. © E.L Fairbanks

TRUST – The Foundation Quality of Leadership in a Community of Faith

As shown in Figure 6.1, trust is the foundation on which we build. Trust is the first component or core quality of Christian Servant Leadership. Likewise, as Christians, our trust in God is fundamental to our beliefs. We trust God. We trust His Word. Trust is presented throughout the Bible as a fundamental characteristic of our relationship with God and Jesus Christ. In Galatians 3:11, Paul writes, "the just shall live by faith"; and in Ephesians 2:8, Paul reaffirms that it is by faith that we accept God's grace. We trust God. Faith and

180

trust are very closely related. Psalm 125:1 compares our trustin the Lord to Mount Zion, "which cannot be shaken but endures forever."

As we all know from past experience from being both the leaders and the led, unless those we are to lead trust us, our effectiveness is doubtful as a Christian leader. The led will allow the leader time to build trust in the leader-led relationship. However, over time, if trust cannot be established, the leader's effectiveness will decline. Furthermore, as Christian leaders, we need to incorporate the thought that trust starts with us. Trust is a two-way street. For the led to trust the leader, the leader must trust the led. We must trust those we are leading.

To explore the concept of trust, I will borrow from the writing of Lovett H. Weems, Jr., former President of Saint Paul School of Theology in Kansas City, Missouri. He now serves as the distinguished professor of church leadership and director of the Lewis Center for Church Leadership at Wesley Theological Seminary in Washington, DC. I want to pursue the topic of trust with an interesting story from Dr. Weems, and then look at trust's three major components according to Dr. Weems: relationships, integrity, and competence.

I heard the seminary leader present this material in October 2001, when 48 leaders, representing business, government, non-profit organizations, academics, and the church, met for three days at the Sandburg Leadership Center on the campus of Ashland Theological Seminary in Ashland, Ohio. Richard Leslie Parrott was the director of the Sandburg Leadership Center at the time of the conference. Dr. Parrott collected papers presented during the three days and published them under the appropriate title, *Leadership Character* (2002). Dr. Parrott now serves as professor of Leadership and Organizational Development, at Trevecca Nazarene University in Nashville, Tennessee.

In his conference presentation, Dr. Weems introduced the idea of "Trust" with the following story and brief introduction included in *Leadership Character* (2002).

> Seminary presidents spend much time raising money. Years ago I heard the statistic that large gifts tend to come after a dozen or so visits, often by the president. I was close to that statistical average with a woman in her nineties. She had ample resources, no family, close ties to the church, interest in our school, yet had never given a single gift. I scheduled yet another visit with her by scheduling a flight with a lengthy layover in her city so I could take her to dinner, as was our usual pattern.
>
> When I arrived at her home, she was not dressed to go out. She indicated that she was not feeling well and perhaps we could visit for a few minutes then I could head back to the airport. We talked briefly in her living room. Then, as we were standing near the door as I was leaving, she said simply, "I trust you." I knew then that we would receive a major gift. She left half of her estate to the seminary for student scholarships.
>
> It became clear to me that people give out of trust and that trust grows out of relationships and experiences that engender such trust (p. 19).

When church leaders begin reading supposedly secular books about leadership, it is often a great surprise that the language used in the best of books seems to come from the vocabulary of the church. Church leaders may expect to find elaborate grids, schemes, and designs.

Instead, the words that dominate have to do with values character, and self-leadership. It soon becomes quite evident that there is no way to talk about leadership without talking about values, meaning, character, and relationships.

Dr. Weems (2002) re-introduced me to a term used in communication theory—"ethical proof" of the speaker. "Ethical proof" refers to the credibility that the hearers accord the speaker. When the ethical proof is high, the task of persuading the audience is not hard. When the ethical proof is neutral, the speaker has a more difficult time. When the ethical proof is extremely negative, the speaker has a very difficult time persuading the audience. This concept means that the way the constituents perceive the leader is probably much more important than the *facts* of the presentation (p. 20).

So it is with the presence of trust and credibility between leaders and constituents. James Kouzes (as cited in Weems, 2002) speaks of credibility as "credit-ability." People are doing an analysis of our credibility all the time just as a bank might assess our credit worthiness. Indeed, credibility is the working capital of the leader. It is the account of credibility that the leader draws on to make possible creative change. Credibility is the foundation upon which all effective leadership builds.

A leader's trust is won very slowly, but it can be lost quickly. Once lost, this trust is very difficult to regain in that leadership setting. People may give us a leadership position through election or employment. However, the credibility needed to lead must be worked out among the people with whom we serve. It is trust from those with whom the leader works most closely that gives a leader the essential element of credibility.

Trust is a constant part of our daily life. We trust the electricity to turn on the switch; we trust traffic signals to control the flow of traffic, the key to turn the tumblers in the lock, and on and on. Regarding relationships, our interaction with co-workers and family members is built on trust. Trust allows us to be productive, efficient. According to Dr. Weems, with low levels of trust, every interaction and exchange would have a "tax" imposed to make progress difficult. Our efficiency would grind to a halt (p. 21).

Leading in non-trusting environments is very difficult. Leading to foster change in those environments is nearly impossible. So as Christian servant leaders, it is essential for us to foster trust in our relationships (pp. 20-21).

Relationships. Relationships feed trust, and trust allows relationships to expand. Trust and relationships grow together. Expanding one requires expanding the other. Deepening relationships requires deepened trust. Relationships were a critical success factor to St. Paul's success in the early stages of Christianity. His experiences and writings showed he built upon existing relationships to lead the church from afar. From Paul's letters we see how deeply he trusted the early Christians and how they must have trusted him. In the context of being Christian leaders within our institutions, whether churches, colleges, or ministry organizations, *relationships* precede plans and programs.

Relationships are critical to successfully executed programs. Leaders may expect tacit acceptance of their leadership in the early stages of relationships; however, the relationship must grow for the group's outcomes to be achieved and for planned programs to succeed. Kouzes and Posner (as cited in Weems, 2002) point out successful leadership is "a reciprocal relationship between those who choose to lead and those who decide to follow" (p. 22).

Lasting trust among those we lead comes from active, day-by-day interaction between the leader and the led, to explore and resolve active issues. That leader-led interaction requires the leader's presence. Thus, an active relationship is vital to building trust. That active presence and interaction between the leader and the led is *communication*. St. Paul traveled widely to visit with the growing church; then, when unable to travel or when an issue needed to be addressed more quickly than he could arrange personally to be on site, he wrote letters and sent emissaries.

Paul truly cared about those in the churches to whom he wrote. Likewise, our care of the led becomes vital for the led to continue investing in the relationship. Caring brings the relationship closer and trust strengthens the relationship. As Weems noted, our success as leaders goes beyond just caring. It achieves the same degree of caring that St. Paul had for the early Christians, it reaches the level of love.

Dr. Martin Luther King, Jr. (as cited by Weems, 2002) said, "Whom you would change, you must first love" (p. 23). Secular writers make the same point in saying "just possibly the best-kept secret of successful leaders is love" (Kouzes & Posner, 1995, p. 305).

So relationships are how trust is developed; and as leaders, we need to be actively engaged, day-by-day, in those relationships. In large organizations where one-to-one relationships are not possible, then we need to insure that people and programs are in place to provide for this care. As in the case of St. Paul, we need to take our caring to the level of love for those we lead.

185

Integrity. Integrity builds trust by having honesty and consistency be a mandatory part of the leaders' words and deeds. Just as faith and works go hand-in-hand and work together, the integrity of our words and actions are indicators of our integrity. Integrity and trust are directly complementary. The lack of integrity erodes trust. Note that integrity is not perfection, rather it is consistency. The leader's words and actions are consistent with each other; they work in concert; and they are complementary.

A story by Lovett Weems (2002) shows how integrity is built by consistency between words and actions. I have had similar experiences, and I assume you have also.

> For a number of years, a United Methodist pastor served in Mississippi with great difficulty. He and his family moved regularly from one modest pastorate to another, sometimes after only one year. The reasons for the frequent moves were many. The educational, personal, and social differences between pastor and assigned congregations were gigantic. However, never far from the surface of parish conflict with their pastor was a profound witness by the pastor against the segregation and racism of the day.
>
> When the United States Supreme Court rendered a decision in late 1969 that finally instituted unitary school systems across the South, this pastor was serving a white congregation in the Mississippi Delta where pronounced African-American population majorities were common. The pastor's community was in a school district affected by the ruling. Within a matter of weeks, whites left the public school system with the exception of the pastor's children.

186

A committee from the church made an appointment with the United Methodist bishop to talk about their pastoral appointment for the coming year. Bishops were accustomed to meeting with delegations upset with this to their particular pastor. However, the bishop was surprised by the delegation's message. They said, "We don't agree or understand what our pastor and his family are doing. However, we respect his commitment to his beliefs. We understand, bishop that it may be best for our pastor's family to move. But, we want you to know that our request to you is that our pastor whom we respect be returned for another year. (p. 23)

In Psalm 25:21, David puts integrity right along with his righteousness as his dual protectors. Jesus spoke about integrity when he told the parable of the master and the dishonest manager. Jesus warned us that being honest with a little is just as important as being honest with much. Furthermore, if we cannot be trusted with worldly wealth, how can we be trusted with "true riches" of God's kingdom (Luke 16: 1-12)? So, as we have heard for many years, we build our own reputation, both with those we lead and with God. For those we lead, we must maintain the highest integrity or consistency between word and deed.

The format for leader-led interaction is relationships; relationships are where trust is built; and integrity (or consistent words and actions) help the leader build the trust of the led. For the evidence of successful servant leadership to occur, the consistent example and power of integrity are required.

Competence. Competence is the third component of trust. Speaking plainly, our followers look to us to be able to accomplish what needs to be done. If we consistently fall short, trust will dissolve. The leader must effectively address the group's current needs.

Trust occurs in and from relationships. Integrity (consistency between words and deeds) is vital to building trust, and competence (the ability to address the organization's needs) is necessary for building long-term trust. As leaders, we know that after an initial "honeymoon" period in any relationship, the led expect the leaders to meet expectations in competence to get the job done. In the religious arena, this expectation takes on additional weight.

As Jackson W. Carroll (2000) points out in *Mainline to the Future*, a study of very large congregations found that their pastoral leaders "establish their authority or right to lead not primarily by virtue of the office they hold or because of their formal credentials, but more by *a combination of demonstrated competence and religious authenticity*" (p. 8). Thus, competence and integrity work together.

A common misconception is for competence to be mistaken for brilliance on the part of the leader. Brilliance or intelligence is not synonymous with competence. Rather, the sought after skill is listening, then analysis, resulting in action to conclusion. It is to hear, to understand, then leading the group to appropriate action. Whether we are aware or not, the led will hold us accountable to address the need. Our ability to address the need successfully is a reflection of our competence. Being competent is helping the group work through the task to successful conclusion. It is not the leader's ability to single-handedly accomplish the task, rather the ability to understand the task and assure the group completes it. In a Christian institutional setting, the leader's competence is demonstrated by the ability to achieve objectives using a collaborative approach so the led accomplish the task.

Another aspect of competence is the ability to stay focused. If achieving the task collaboratively is desirable, then the leader's job is to keep the group focused on the task until successfully accomplished. Doing so is competence. This focus must be coupled with appropriate action and a working knowledge of the task at hand. Competence requires the leader to become familiar with the task at hand, even if the leader does not personally perform the work. Competence is listening and focused action. Competence requires work on the part of the leader.

Trust, vision, and leadership. Trust alone does not make leadership, especially Christian leadership. Reflecting back on a basic tenet of this book, how does the life of Christ change how we carry out our roles as leaders?

Christ's leadership coupled a strong vision with trust to be a strong leader. Like Him, the successful Christian servant leader must couple vision to trust. Without vision, the leader becomes a manager of the status quo. With vision and trust, the leader moves the led forward. Vision with passion and commitment inspire the people being led. Vision transforms inanimate trust into a living, effective leadership. The New Testament shows repeatedly how Jesus Christ continually portrayed vision passionately to inspire his followers. Christ worked tirelessly at this. By His example, we see that being a leader requires vision and passion, and they are conveyed by energy. Vision and inspiration require work. Vision with passion, commitment, and dedication inspire the led to achieve beyond what they anticipated.

However, we must keep in mind what we learned in chapters three, four, and five. In these chapters on GOAL, METHOD and PAIN, we were reminded that being a leader is disciplined work. Among the many responsibilities of the leader, maintaining the balance between trust and vision is one the Christian leader must tirelessly maintain. The leader with trust and no vision administers or maintains the status quo. The leader with vision and no trust will have a short tenure as leader, as the leader needs the led. A leader abandoned by the led is no longer leading.

The example of Jesus as an inspirational leader with a vision is an interesting example and role model, when attempting to develop servant leadership qualities and characteristics. Jesus passionately declared a singular vision to a heterogeneous community at the crossroads of the Mediterranean world. His vision was a radical departure from the conventional wisdom of the Jewish faith and its various groups as well as the Roman culture. Yet, with inspired vision that reached beyond the world known to his followers, He was able to be the ultimate leader and the ultimate servant.

Following the example of Jesus, the vision to transform trust into leadership need not be complex. Repeatedly, Jesus' disciples and apostles communicated a simple vision to the new church: Accept Jesus into your heart to be saved. In the case of our being the servant leader, our vision should be equally simple and straightforward. The vision should be short and very easy for anyone among the led to explain.

Vision brings trust alive. Vision is the propellant of trust. Likewise, trust is the harness of vision. Vision passionately pursued can exceed the bounds placed on it by trust, the trust earned from integrity and competence and developed in relationships. Vision can become its own master. We have all seen examples of this happening where the vision exceeds the bounds placed on it by the trust of the led. Jesus speaks directly to this risk in the

Beatitudes (Matthew 5:3-12), especially verse 5, "Blessed are the meek, for they will inherit the earth." No leader is exempt from the accountability of his flock. This is especially true for the servant leader. The leader's drive and vision must never exceed the trust placed on the leader by the led, such that the trust is expendable in favor of achieving the vision.

Brokenness: The Core Quality That Purifies Our Ambitions

"For you, O God, tested us; you refined us like silver. You brought us into prison and laid burdens on our backs. You let men to ride over our heads; we went through fire and water, but you brought us to a place of abundance" (Psalm 66:10-12).

Brokenness is the second core quality on which leading decisively is built. The relationship between brokenness and leadership in the real world of the local church or in a Christian university often presents conflicting expectations and multiple demands for the leader. In these situations, how do we lead Christianly, consistently, and with vision and courage? In these ministry assignments, how can we lead decisively when we feel abused, manipulated, undermined, and ignored? And if God has permitted words to be spoken or deeds to be done against us, why? What does He want to teach you...and me? What does He want to teach others? What is the relationship between pastoral leadership and the brokenness of spirit we often experience in these situations?

Wesley often used this Covenant Prayer at the beginning of each New Year.

I am no longer my own, but Yours.
Put me to what You will,
Rank me with whom You will.
Put me to doing, put me to suffering.
Let me be employed by You or laid aside for You.
Exalted for You or brought low by You.
Let me have all things, let me have nothing.
I freely and heartily yield all things to
Your pleasure and disposal.
And now, O glorious and blessed God,
Father, Son, and Holy Spirit,
You are mine, and I am Yours.
So be it.
And the covenant which I have made on earth,
Let it be ratified in heaven. Amen.

What in John Wesley's prayer did you hear? Did you hear the words "Suffering…laid aside for you…brought low by you…have nothing…disposal…?" Those are the descriptors of a broken heart.

What is the relationship between brokenness (as described by Wesley) and Christ-like or servant leadership? How can one effectively lead from the posture of a "wounded" leader? How should one lead "with a broken heart"? How can the servant leader hope for the desired results of qualitative change among the led, the evidence of leadership, "with a broken heart"?

Brokenness is one of those intangibles that is easier to recognize when it is experienced but more difficult to describe. Brokenness is not the same as humility, but brokenness leads us to humility. Brokenness varies in degrees from uncomfortable to seemingly unbearable emotional pain. Sometimes, God uses brokenness when He needs to get our attention — wherever we happen to be in our walk with Him. Such was the case with Job and his trials.

192

Sometimes things happen that are outside of our control. God does not cause the circumstances; however, He allows them to happen. God can use our brokenness to draw us closer to Him. He uses brokenness brought on by others to draw us closer to Him. Listen to Psalms 51:16-17— *"The sacrifices of God are a broken spirit, a broken and contrite heart. These, O God, You will not despise."* God's process of helping us develop character involves being broken before Him.

What are the character qualities God wants to form in us (often through brokenness)? *"For this reason, make every effort to add to your faith goodness; and to goodness, knowledge; and to knowledge, self-control; and to self-control, perseverance; and to perseverance, godliness; and to godliness, brotherly kindness; and to brotherly kindness, love. For if you possess these qualities in increasing measure, they will keep you from being ineffective and unproductive in your knowledge of our Lord Jesus Christ. But if anyone does not have them, he is nearsighted and blind, and has forgotten that he has been cleansed from his past sins"* (II Peter 1:5-9).

In the book, *Broken in the Right Place: How God Tames the Soul*, Nelson (1994) made some powerful statements regarding brokenness:

Brokenness purifies our ambitions.
Brokenness allows us to see our own blind spots.
We cast stones at others," he says,
"out of our blind spots."
The breaking process produces a leader that can be trusted (p. 7).

Nelson (1994) quoted Korean mega-church pastor Paul Cho, "I have yet to see a leader God has used tremendously who has not been broken" (p. 7)

The following questions assist us as we respond to these attitude checks for brokenness. Our daily responses to these questions characterize us at our best and convict us at our worst.

1. Am I willing to let go of my dreams and ambitions if such is God's will?

2. Am I defensive when accused, criticized, or misunderstood?

3. Am I coveting what others have instead of waiting for heaven's rewards?

4. Am I forgiving when offended, with or without apology?

5. Am I complaining or arguing out of unsurrendered rights?

6. Am I thinking of others first out of love?

7. Am I proudly appearing that I am always right or know all the answers?

8. Am I practicing the spiritual disciplines (prayer, fasting, solitude, simplicity)?

9. Am I being silent regarding self-promotion?

10. Am I daily saying, "God, whatever it takes, I'm willing to submit to Your leadership?

11. Am I expressing joy in the difficulties, which serve to refine me?

12. Am I taking risks out of obedience to Christ instead of giving into fear, pride, or denial?

Remember, a leader who allows herself/himself to go through the breaking process produces a leader that can be trusted.

What are the *fruits* of brokenness? No one wants to be broken. Why is it necessary for Christian leaders to be broken? The fruits of brokenness are humility, authenticity, integrity, and sensitivity. All of these qualities are desirable as a leader. Let's focus more closely on the "fruit" of *humility* as a part of brokenness.

Humility is another word difficult to define but necessary if the leader is to be effective. Remember Ephesians 4:1-2: *"As a prisoner for the Lord, then, I urge you to live a life worthy of the calling you have received. Be completely humble and gentle, be patient, bearing with one another in love."* In Proverbs 15:22, we read: *"Before honor is humility."*

In biblical perspective, humility is a prerequisite to the things we seek most in our lives. Listen to these seven ways — very common ways — to spot a humble spirit.

Humility does not demand its own way.
Humility exudes an attitude of service
(service is doing mundane things that help others).
Humility does not seek attention or credit.
Humility forgives when offended,
but is hard to offend.
Humility does not criticize others.
Humility produces a teachable spirit.
Humility is gracious and thankful.

In fact, one of the most Godlike attributes we can express is a gracious spirit — a spirit of mercy and thanksgiving. (Nelson 1994).

Romans 12:21 states that *"humble servants overcome evil with good."* The paragraph heading for the great *kenosis* passage, Philippians 2:1-11, is "Imitating Christ's Humility." It reads:

If you have any encouragement from being united with Christ, if any comfort from his love, if any fellowship with the Spirit, if any tenderness and compassion, then make my joy complete by being like-minded, having the same love, being one in spirit and purpose. Do nothing out of selfish ambition or vain conceit, but in humility consider others better than yourselves. Each of you should look not only to your own interests, but also to the interests of others. Your attitude should be the same as that of Christ Jesus: Who, being in very nature God, did not consider equality with God something to be grasped, but made himself nothing, taking the very nature of a servant, being made in human likeness. And being found in appearance as a man, he humbled himself and became obedient to death — even death on a cross! Therefore God exalted him to the highest place and gave him the name that is above every name, that at the name of Jesus every knee should bow, in heaven and on earth and under the earth, and every tongue confess that Jesus Christ is Lord, to the glory of God the Father.

We can respond in one of two ways to the brokenness in our lives. We can resent the situation, person, circumstance, or God and grow bitter, become angry, and withdraw. Or, we can be driven to our knees to ask God what He wants to teach us through the brokenness. We need to learn certain things about ourselves if we are to grow and mature in the faith and our calling. In turn, this will nurture the character qualities needed as servant leaders and our ability to achieve the goal of qualitative change among the led, the evidence of servant leadership.

God often uses people who are different from us, people with whom we have problems, to teach us these lessons we need to know about ourselves. As strong as we think we are, we recognize how weak we really are, and how much we need our heavenly Father if we are to lead in the way He wants us to lead. Too often it seems that we are driven to our knees with the words of II Corinthians 12:9: *But he said to me, "My grace is sufficient for you, for my power is made perfect in weakness."*

The words of this contemporary song remind us of the truth of this passage.

> *His strength is perfect when our strength is gone,*
> *He'll carry us when we can't carry on,*
> *Raised in His power, the weak become strong,*
> *His strength is perfect, His strength is perfect.*
> (Lyrics and music by Stephen Curtis Chapman)

Therefore, we are to respond as Christian leaders…

- by yielding responsibility of the "led" to the Christ who indwells within us by His Spirit

- by living in, through, and from the spiritual disciplines of prayer, Bible study, and solitude

- by living a "grace" filled life

- by focusing on our walk and relationship with Christ, and not on others and their expectations.

- by leading pastorally out of the pain and brokenness (not denying it).

- by acknowledging our weaknesses, and our total dependency upon the Christ who indwell within by His Spirit. He is the One who will empower, guide, and comfort the pastor and other leaders who seek to lead out of their brokenness.

- by expecting trials, temptations, verbal abuse, misunderstandings, rejection, and a sense of being "used" by some whom we are suppose to lead.

- by relating to those in the Christian fellowship who profess faith in Christ as brothers and sisters in Christ (even though evidence may not support their testimony).

Read again Wesley's Covenant Prayer.

The prayer of Saint Francis of Assisi embodies the *spirit* of the broken leader of Psalm 66. Let me pray this prayer for you and for me, as we seek to lead in ways that strengthen the faith in the led:

Lord, make me an instrument of Thy peace;
Where there is hatred, let me sow love;
Where there is injury, pardon;
Where there is doubt, faith;
Where there is despair, hope;
Where there is darkness, light;
Where there is sadness, joy.
O Divine Master, grant that I may not so much seek
To be consoled as to console,
To be understood as to understand,
To be loved as to love;
For it is in giving that we receive;
It is in pardoning that we are pardoned;
It is in dying that we are born to eternal life.

How can we lead when we feel abused, ignored, manipulated?

1. Am I willing to see my brokenness?

2. Am I willing to bring my brokenness to God and allow Him to bring about transformation?

3. How will brokenness help me become a more effective servant leader?

Practicing the Core Quality of Gratefulness

I first heard the words to the chorus "**Give Thanks**" in 1989, when I attended the Lausanne Congress on World Evangelization in Manila, Philippines. You may know the words.

Give thanks with a grateful heart;
Give thanks to the Holy One;
Give thanks because He's given Jesus Christ, His Son.
And now let the weak say, "I am strong,"
Let the poor say, "I am rich,"
Because of what the Lord has done for us. Give thanks.
Words and music by Henry Smith, 1978

Five thousand delegates from 192 countries participated in the 10-day conference. At the time of the conference, the Berlin Wall stood firm. The Central and Eastern Europe Soviet bloc remained in tact. Numerous African countries were involved in civil wars.

Yet, I heard testimonies of God's grace from delegates from these and other countries where Christians were regularly persecuted. I was profoundly impacted.

These believers accepted I Thessalonians 5:18 as an imperative and a way of life for them. *"Give thanks in all circumstances for this is God's will for you in Christ Jesus."*

Two weeks later, July 27, 1989, to be exact, I was elected president of Mount Vernon Nazarene College. For several reasons, Anne and I hesitated to accept the call. We were fearful that we would forget some core values of the Filipino Christians. The Filipino Christians with whom we worked were such grateful people. They prayed often for daily bread and were so free to express gratitude to God and to others for the numerous blessings (a word frequently used by Filipino Christians). Anne and I did not want to return to the States and get caught up in the cynicism, sarcasm, materialism, negativism, and criticism we felt was so pervasive in America at the time.

Eleven years later, the 2000 academic year was a wake-up call for me. I began the year feeling as if I had been sucked into the very lifestyle and mindset that I detested 11 years earlier. It came to a head for me in October, when I heard Brennan Manning during MVNU's Estep Prayer Lecture Series.

In his chapel message, Manning asked, "Let's say I interviewed 10 people, asking each the question—'Do you trust God?' and each answered, 'Yes, I trust God,' but 9 of the 10 actually did NOT trust Him. How would I find out which one of the professing Christians was telling the truth?" He continued, "I would videotape each of the 10 lives for a month and then, after watching the videos, pass judgment using this criterion: The person with an abiding spirit of gratitude is the one who trusts God."

The scriptures remind us that God desires a thankful people, a grateful people, not a murmuring, grumbling, faultfinding, and complaining people.

However, in our real world of living and leading within the Christian community, how can we recapture a spirit of gratitude as we work daily with problems, people, and the conflicting perspectives of those whom we serve?

Will we live as faithful disciples with consistently grateful hearts in the difficult situations we face and the multiple demands placed on us in present and future leadership assignments? I passionately desire that each of us have a renewed commitment to cultivate a spirit of gratefulness in our lives. How can we recapture a spirit of gratitude as a way of living? Listen again to I Thessalonians 5:18: "*Give thanks in all circumstances, for this is God's will for you in Christ Jesus.*"

TO WALK IN GRATITUDE AS A WAY OF LIVING, the text reminds us, our gratitude must be: ATTENTIVE ("Give thanks."), INCLUSIVE ("In all circumstances"), and GOD-CENTERED ("For this is God's will in Christ Jesus.").

Let's look more carefully at each one of these imperatives of gratefulness or gratitude, the third core quality upon which successful servant leadership is built. The three imperatives of gratitude—Attentive, Inclusive, and God-Centered—are essential for a consistently **grateful** Christian and, therefore, servantleader.

Our gratitude must be attentive. "*Give thanks*"—(I Thessalonians 5:18a). Do you recall the story in Luke 17 of the 10 lepers cleansed by Jesus? Ten were cleansed; yet, only one of the cleansed lepers returned to Jesus to thank him. Were the other nine not aware they had been cleaned?

Attentiveness to what God is doing enables us to "see" and "focus" through the "eyes of our eyes"—our spiritual eyes.

We look for the miracles and marvels of God in our lives — our equivalent to the crossing of the Red Sea, the pillar of fire by night, and the manna by day, the daily protections from our *enemies*, or the *healing* of our leprosy! With this attentiveness comes gratitude to Him who promised never to leave or forsake us! God really is for us!

When we are continually preoccupied with busyness, the tyranny of the urgent, and the incessant running to meet everyone's expectations, then our thoughts cannot be focused. In my own flurry of activities, Manning caught my attention when he repeated, rather loudly, I recall, "Awareness, awareness, awareness, awareness...."

A Spirit-empowered attentiveness to God alerts us to the Presence of God manifested in a piece of music, a bird, a daffodil, a kiss, an encouraging word from a friend, a thunderstorm, a newborn baby, a fresh blanket of snow, a full moon, a sunrise, a sunset, or a rainbow.

There are gifts of God we often take for granted. What about the grace-gifts from individuals — people with whom we live, work, or worship — colleagues and friends on this campus or in local churches? And what about our family members and fellow employees...or even employers? Are we attentive to the small and large gifts God gives us through people close to us! Or are we taking them for granted...always expecting more? In the southeastern part of the United States, where Anne and I grew up, should you spend any time with the older Christians, you would not help but notice how often they say, "Thank you, Jesus."

To be aware and alert to the Presence of God manifested in the predictability of a job or the unpredictability of the people with whom we live and work requires a spirit-empowered attentiveness to God.

From this perspective, the difficult people with whom we work, the conflicting expectations placed on us, the multiple demands and the sheer exhaustion we experience can be placed in perspective. Through attentiveness to God's activities in our lives, the people around us and the place we work can become a source of joy—abiding joy— in the midst of seemingly impossible situations. The Spirit of God within us enables us through attentiveness to give thanks. Our gratitude must be attentive.

Our gratitude must be inclusive. Our gratitude must be "in all circumstances"—(I Thessalonians 5:18b). Job asks, "If we take happiness from God's hand, must we not take sorrow, too?" Nouwen (2009) wrote in an article of the spiritual work of gratitude:

> To be grateful for the good things that happen in our lives is easy, but to be grateful for all of our lives—the good as well as the bad, the moments of joy as well as the moments of sorrow, the successes as well as the failures, the rewards as well as the rejections—that requires hard spiritual work. Still, we are only grateful people when we can say thank you to all that has brought us to the present moment. As long as we keep dividing our lives between events and people we would like to remember and those we would rather forget, we cannot claim the fullness of our beings as a gift of God to be grateful for.(Legacy.blogspot.com/2009/01/SpiritualWorkofGratitude.html)

Do not focus just on the circumstances you normally would call wonderful. God may use difficult circumstances in a wonderful way. So we thank Him in the difficult circumstances, also! Manning (2000) told the story of a grateful, old woman in an extended care hospital:

She had some kind of 'wasting' disease, her powers fading away over the march of the month. A student worker spoke to her on a coincidental visit. The student kept going back, drawn by the strange force of a woman's joy. Though she could no longer move her arms and legs, the elderly lady would say, "I'm just so happy I can move my neck." When she could no longer move her neck, she would say, "I'm just so glad I can hear and see." When the young student finally asked the old woman what would happen if she lost sound and sight, the gentle old lady said, "I'll just be so grateful that you come to visit." (presented in a chapel service at Mount Vernon Nazarene University)

Remember to be thankful, grateful, for all things, including the little things.

Jesus said, "...*whosoever can be trusted with very little can be trusted with much...*" (Luke 16:10). If you are grateful in small things, even in a small way, you will naturally express gratitude in great things. Remember the ten lepers. For whatever reason, 9 of the 10 cleansed lepers chose not to return to give thanks.

The discipline of giving thanks in all circumstances is so painful and difficult at times, especially when we have been hurt deeply. But I am learning to say, "Thank you God even in these times for the lessons You are teaching me about myself, my relationship to you, and others." Nouwen (1974) speaks of an old priest who told him, "My whole life I have been complaining that my work was constantly interrupted until I discovered that my interruptions were my work" (p. 56).

Our gratitude must be inclusive—the joy and the sorrow, the small blessings as well as the large gifts from

God, the interruptions and the routine. *"Give thanks in all circumstances..."* (I Thessalonians 5:18b). This does not mean that we are grateful for sin and the causes of sin. The Spirit of God may prompt us to step away from those who would tempt us with a sinning lifestyle, even as we express gratitude for those individuals as creations of God for whom Christ died.

Our gratitude must be God-centered. I Thessalonians 5:18c admonishes us, that this is the will of God for us in Christ Jesus.

The theocentric or God-centered character of gratitude is anchored in ruthless trust that there is a God who is Sovereign and whose providential care guides His people. By divine mercy, we have been given the unearned gift of salvation. We received this gift through no merit of our own. Our sins have been forgiven though the blood of Jesus Christ.

When we celebrate the reality that we have received a gift we can never repay; we notify others with our faces and our actions. The tenor of our lives becomes one of humble and joyful thanksgiving. We rejoice in the gift. *"Give thanks to the Lord for He is good, his love is everlasting"* (Psalms 107:1). *"Now thanks be to God for His gift [of grace]"* (II Corinthians 9:15).

An MVNU faculty member whose testimony reflected these passages spoke to me following a chapel service. She said, "I am learning new ways to see life and work as a means to express gratitude to God for his grace, mercy, and faithfulness" (personal communication, 2001). I wrote down her words, they were so impacting on me. New ways to see life and work! *That* is gratefulness!

God reminds me over and over again that the foremost quality of a trusting disciple and a Christian leader is gratefulness. Gratitude arises from the acceptance of all of life as grace — as an undeserved and unearned gift — a Grace gift — from the Father's hand. And God has reminded me that gratitude is grounded in a focus on God and His mercy and grace, and not in a preoccupation with people and their problems. I state this with conviction because the opposite of gratitude is, of course, ingratitude; and the antithesis of giving thanks is grumbling.

Ingratitude is one of the most grievous of sins and it should be detested. Why? For it is a forgetting of the graces, benefits, and blessings received. Remember ingratitude and negative attitudes were among the Israelites major problems and caused them to wander in the wilderness for 40 years before entering the Promised Land.

Grumblers are like a crew of vineyard workers who had labored from dawn to dusk and felt cheated when the latecomers received the same wage (Matthew 20:1-16). Grumblers bellyache about the unfairness of life, the poverty of their resources, the insensitivity of their spouse or employer, the liberals, the conservatives, the hot weather, the cold weather, the rich, the poor, the inadequate administrator of a Christian university, and the incompetent pastor of the local church. Grumblers bellyache! Gratitude, however, is not grounded in murmuring, grumbling, faultfinding, or complaining; but gratitude is found in the conviction that God is big enough to handle any situation we encounter!

I have come to see in a profound way that it is *gratitude* that makes us joyful, not the other way around. Too often, we are not grateful to God because we are sad when things do not go our way. Slowly, very slowly but surely. I am coming to see that joy does not make us

206

grateful. Rather it is gratitude that makes us joyful.

As a Christian leader, a servant leader, do you find it difficult to imagine that gratefulness can become the basic attitude of your life? This will only be possible when your gratefulness is Attentive ("Give thanks..."), Inclusive ("In all circumstances...") and God-Centered ("For this is the will of God in Christ Jesus").

The challenge for servant leaders who desire to make a profound and qualitative difference and, thus, achieve the evidence of effective servant leadership in the lives of the led is this: Give thanks to God in the midst of the most difficult situations. This is the foundation of a spiritual life needed to sustain you and me during the months and years ahead. Do not let routines of life dull you to the surprises of God!

Give thanks with a grateful heart. Let us all say , "I will be a consistently, grateful Christian," because of what the Lord has done for me!

1. How does gratefulness as servant leaders enhance our ministry?

2. How can we "give thanks" at all times?

3. Toward whom have I recently shown gratitude?

Hospitality: Making Room...the Creation of Friendly Space

During one Christmas season while Anne and I were serving in Mount Vernon, we spent a fascinating evening in Columbus with a former MVNU student and his girlfriend. We walked to a nearby restaurant to purchase some Chinese food. We ate the meal by candlelight while sitting on the floor in a circle. The meal was great. The three-hour discussion was phenomenal. What a great blessing to Anne and me as well as to the other couple! Sharing our meal. Sharing our time. Sharing our journey. During the evening, Anne and I experienced what the Bible refers to as hospitality.

This fourth core quality in leading decisively, *hospitality*, was a way of life fundamental to Christian identity for seventeen hundred years of the Christian church. Christine Pohl (1999) convincingly documented this practice in her book, *Making Room: Recovering Hospitality in Christian Tradition*.

Embracing the rich concept of biblical hospitality is a lifelong pursuit, as hospitality becomes part of the servant leader seeking to achieve qualitative impact on those being led. Hospitality has the potential of transforming relationships with those individuals with whom we live and work.

I have wrestled with the biblical and historic understanding of hospitality in the Christian tradition including its pain, limitations, and the leadership implications. Here, I simply want to address the fundamental concept of spiritual hospitality.

Biblically and theologically, the term *hospitality* is not limited to receiving a stranger into our homes, although it surely includes this dimension. Fundamentally, it is a core *attitude* toward those we are leading. This hospitality can be expressed by a variety of behaviors. Hospitality, biblically understood, challenges us to relate to others *as if* we were relating to Christ Himself. "Hospitality" means primarily the creation of free space, or "making room," making room, to use Pohl's words, (1999) where the strange and the stranger can enter and become friends. It is being to others with whom you live and work, a "living witness of the risen Christ." The gift of Christian hospitality is the opportunity we provide the guest, the stranger, or the friend to find his or her own way, even in the context of differences of thought or behavior.

With this perspective, the attitude of hospitality helps us to make room or create space for those with whom we live and work. It often provides the opportunity for those individuals to enter into deeper contact with others and with God. The result is often a healing relationship and the creation of a faith *community*.

Hospitality, seeks to offer friendship without binding the other, unity without artificiality, freedom without leaving the person alone, faith without cajoling or demeaning, and respect for individual differences. It is an art and discipline that Christians need to cultivate.

A pastor talked to me recently regarding a couple with whom a misunderstanding had developed with him. The couple had left the church. My words to the pastor, "Give them space." He did, and they responded to the grace their pastor had extended to them. He called me a few days ago and told me of a wonderful reconciliation between pastor and couple.

Let me share with you two insights into this fascinating challenge of "spiritual hospitality." Spiritual hospitality flows to and from Christ. As we exercise our servant leadership, we maintain an open channel between ourselves (the leaders) and the led, and between Christ and ourselves. Hospitality goes in two directions—*from* Christ and us to the led, and *to* us from the led and Christ.

Firstly, the gift of "spiritual hospitality" is a "love gift" to Christ. The passage Colossians 3:17, 23-24 reminds us that our service to others is service to the Lord Christ. This concept is at the very core of servant leadership. In our efforts we can be hurt, misunderstood, and rejected; or we can be appreciated, affirmed, and accepted. The response, however, does not dictate our action. We love because He first loved us.

When Anne and I moved to Manila, Philippines, both of us were overwhelmed by the pervasiveness of poverty in the country. Anne shared her despair with a Filipino friend, a female dentist. Anne's friend encouraged her to focus on the few she could help, not on the masses she could not. Anne took her advice and focused on some women in need around us. She bought glasses for one lady, new teeth for another, and for another she sponsored a beautician's course and attended the graduation ceremony. Anne befriended these ladies and invited them often to our home. By serving those few, she was serving Christ.

Our small tasks are translated by grace into God's great work. This is the mystery of hospitality. Service to others through hospitality, biblically understood, is service to Christ. Consider the concluding words from Matthew 25. *"The King will reply, 'I tell you the truth, whatever you did for one of the least of these brothers of mine, you did for me.'"*

Our gifts of hospitality to others are not selective "spiritual gifts" given by God to only a few for use in the kingdom. Rather, our gifts of care and concern to others are practical expressions of our love for Christ. For sure, with the commitment to a lifestyle of "spiritual hospitality," key questions come to each of us:

1. What can I do to be hospitable in leading others? Where can I be hospitable?

210

2. How will my attitude of hospitality impact the way I live, learn, and lead?

3. How do I deal with my unfinished agenda for the day when I attempt to "create space" and make room for others and in so doing *not* accomplish what I think needs to get done?

These are real life questions with which we must grapple. Spiritual hospitality takes time, patience, and understanding.

Consider the old Sufi story of a "watermelon hunter" (Shah, as cited in Kopp, 1972).

Once upon a time, there was a man who strayed from his own country into the world known as the Land of Fools. He soon saw a number of people fleeing in terror from a field where they had been trying to reap wheat. "There is a monster in that field," they told him. He looked and saw that it was a watermelon.

He offered to kill the "monster" for them. When he had cut the melon from its stalk, he took a slice and began to eat it. To his amazement, the people became even more terrified of him than they had been of the melon. They drove him away with pitchforks crying, "He will kill us next, unless we get rid of him."

It so happened that at another time another man also strayed into the Land of Fools, and the same thing started to happen to him. But, instead of offering to help them with the "monster," he agreed with them that it must be dangerous and by tiptoeing away from it with them he gained their

211

confidence. He spent a long time with them in their houses until he could teach them, little by little, the basic facts, which would enable them not only to lose their fear of melons, but even to cultivate them themselves. (p. 8)

With which "hunter" do you most identify? The second hunter was the servant leader. By solidarity with the led, trying to understand their concerns and spending quality time with them, the second "hunter" made a profound difference in the lives of the people in the story. He made a qualitative change in the lives of the led. His evidence was how they dramatically changed their perspective on melons. **He "made room" and "created space" for these people who were different from him.** Remember, we serve Christ through "practicing hospitality." In so doing, we assist others in *their* growth and maturity in Christ. Again, the gift of spiritual hospitality is a love gift *to* Christ.

Secondly, the "gift of spiritual hospitality" is a love gift from Christ. The miracle of miracles is that *we* are blessed when we reach out to others. Christ turns our "gifts of hospitality" to others into "gifts" from Him to us. We find our *Lord* in the midst of our service to *others.* How often we experience God's abiding presence in the midst of our very ordinary expressions of "making room and creating space for those with whom we live and work."

Nouwen (1985b) defined compassionate actions or spiritual hospitality as "being to *others* what Saint John was for his listeners and readers: A living *witness* of the risen Christ" (Nouwen, 1985b). Something happens *to us* and *in us* as we reach out to others with gifts of hospitality. Thus, a qualitative change occurs in the servant leader as well as in the led. The grace of Christ flows to us and through us when we work, play, and study with the mind of Christ!

Our tendency, however, is to hesitate because we feel our "gifts" are so insignificant. Brennan Manning (2000) shared this applicable story in an MVNU chapel service about "The Cracked Pot."

A water bearer in India had two large pots. Each hung on opposite ends of a pole that he carried across his neck. One of the pots had a crack in it, while the other was perfect. The latter always delivered a full portion of water at the end of the long walk from the stream to the master's house. The cracked pot arrived only half-full. Every day for two full years, the water bearer delivered only one and a half pots of water.

The perfect pot was proud of its accomplishments, because it fulfilled magnificently the purpose for which it had been made. But the poor cracked pot was ashamed of its imperfection, miserable that it was to accomplish only half of what it had been made to do.

After the second year of what it perceived to be a bitter failure, the unhappy pot spoke to the water bearer one day by the stream. "I am ashamed of myself, and I want to apologize to you," the pot said.

"Why?" asked the bearer. "What are you ashamed of?"

"I have been able, for these past two years, to deliver only half my load, because this crack in my side causes water to leak out all the way back to your master's house. Because of my flaws, you have to do all this work and you don't get full value from your efforts," the pot said.

The water bearer felt sorry for the old cracked pot, and in his compassion, he said, "As we return to the master's house, I want you to notice the beautiful flowers along the path." Indeed, as they went up the hill, the cracked pot took notice of the beautiful wildflowers on the side of the path, bright in the sun's glow, and the sight cheered it up a bit.

But at the end of the trail, it still felt bad that it had leaked out half its load, and so again it apologized to the bearer for its failure.

The bearer said to the pot, "Did you notice that there were flowers only on your side of the path, not on the other pot's side? That is because I have always known about your flaw, and I have taken advantage of it. I planted flower seeds on your side of the path, and every day, as we have walked back from the stream you have watered them. For two years I have been able to pick these beautiful flowers to decorate my master's table. Without you being just the way you are, he would not have had this beauty to grace his house." (A story from India-author unknown)

In our efforts at spiritual hospitality, do we sometimes feel like the "cracked pot?" Yes! But, God has a way of using our availability and our efforts toward others in ways we could never imagine. And in the process, He blesses us in ways we never dreamed possible!

Again, the gift of hospitality — this gift of creating space and making room for others — by grace alone, becomes a love gift *from* Christ to *us*. *We* grow and mature in our faith as we increasingly "practice hospitality." Remember, the miracle of miracles is that *we* are blessed when we reach out to others in Jesus' name.

Let me remind you that, fundamentally, hospitality in Christian perspective is much more than being nice and feeding friends. It is a *way* of *life* for believers and dictates how we approach those with whom we live, work, and serve. For the strangers, the disenfranchised and lonely, our family members and friends, creating space and making room for them—this is the essence of hospitality, biblically understood. Yet, *we* experience the "surprises of God" in *our* lives in the process of enabling *others* to grow and mature. Through "providing space" and "making room" for others to grow, *we* are given "space" by God to grow and mature in Christ-likeness.

Hospitality, biblically understood, is nothing less than the amazing grace of God working **in** us and **through** us! Let's pursue this nearly forgotten practice in Christian tradition. Join me in seeking to discover the rich implications of "spiritual hospitality," especially as it relates to those with whom we work (or will work!). May each of you increasingly become that jar of clay for others, and in the process be shaped and reshaped by the Potter's hand.

Am I willing to be hospitable to individuals who differ and sometimes collide with me?

If hospitality brings about community, whom do you place in the "poor section of town" in your mind?

Who doesn't "fit" with "us" in your mind?

How does the hospitality I receive from Christ make me a more effective servant leader?

Compassion: Enabling Others to See What They Have Not Seen in Themselves

The fifth core quality of the decisive leader, **Compassion,** is nearly synonymous with caring in the context of qualities of the servant leader. Our compassion, or care, for others can be intimate or distant.

What do we mean by "care"? The word "care" finds its root in the Celtic term "kara," which means lament. The basic meaning of care is "to grieve, to experience sorrow, to cry out with" (Nouwen, McNeil, & Morrison, 1983, p. 92). The background of the word "care" strikes me because we tend to look at caring of the strong toward the weak, of the powerful toward the powerless, of the "haves" toward the "have-nots."

I am coming to understand that biblical compassion is not a skill that we acquire. Rather, it is a quality of the human heart that must be revealed. The late Henri Nouwen (1983) often stated that you cannot get a Ph.D. in caring (p. 90). Nouwen helped me to realize that when we see the other person and discover in that person gentleness, tenderness, and other beautiful gifts, which he or she is not able to see, then our compassionate heart is revealed!

What a profound thought! **Our compassionate heart is revealed as we enable others to see what they have not, nor cannot, see in themselves!** Again, we see the reciprocal, two-way part of servant leadership. As Christian servant leaders, we become conduits of God's caring or compassion. We are talking about caring relationships with people, the people we lead as servant leaders. The "evidence" of our leadership is in equipping and enabling others to see what they have not seen in themselves. To be compassionate is not, first of all, something we do for others, but rather it is discovering with others *their* divinely given resources and inner qualities. It is a way of being present with others and standing with them in their times of need. I am slowly coming to see that God wants us to be *with* others...not to prove that we are valuable to them.

When we honestly ask ourselves which persons in our lives mean the most to us, we often find that it is those who, instead of giving much advice, solutions, or cures, have chosen rather to share our pain and touch our wounds with a gentle and tender hand. The friend who can be silent with us in a moment of despair or confusion — who can stay with us in an hour of grief and bereavement, who can tolerate not knowing, not curing, not healing, and not doing — that is the friend who cares.

You may remember moments, as I do, in which we were called to be with a friend who had lost a brother, a sister, a wife or husband, child or parent. What can we say, do, or propose at such a moment? There is a strong inclination to say things such as, "Don't cry; the one you loved is in the hands of God." or "Don't be sad because there are so many good people and so many good things left worth living for." "Caring deeply" in these moments demands that we *listen* intently, speak directly and caringly, and ask questions for the *other* person's sake and not for our own. We are truly present, even in the quietness; and we pray honestly, openly, and confidently!

Nouwen, McNeil, and Morrison (1983) introduced me to the phenomenal concept of voluntary displacement (pp. 62-74) in their book entitled *Compassion: A Reflection on the Christian Life*. Voluntary displacement means that for the sake of others, we willingly go to places we had rather not go. We move out of our comfort zones voluntarily and "displace" ourselves outside the familiar.

217

Why? A need exists; a response from within is required; an inward call from God is felt; we go, because of who we are. Voluntary displacement can take us to the inner city or around the world. This calling can be for a brief time or for a lifetime.

Nouwen's life illustrated how caring deeply for others often interrupts our routines of life. It really was not difficult for Nouwen to leave his teaching positions at Notre Dame, Harvard, and Yale divinity schools to accept an invitation to spend the final ten years of his life living and working as priest to the L'Arche Community for the severely mentally handicapped in Toronto. His specific daily responsibility was to care for Adam. It took Nouwen two hours each day to prepare Adam for breakfast.

Care deeply. Be deeply compassionate. Our care for others can be intimate or distant.

1. As a pastor director, or university president, how can I express compassion appropriately in my servant leadership to members of the opposite sex?

2. How can I increasingly make compassion central to my leadership ministry?

Endurance: Staying with the Assignment God Has Given to You

A Salvation Army officer who graduated from the MVNU Master of Ministry program wrote to me following a class I taught. Among other comments, she stated, "I cannot get away from the discussion of Paul's admonition to Archippus in Colossians 4:17. *"Do not walk away from the assignment God has given you."*

She continued, "The hardest orders I have received have been those to stay in my assignment and continue God's work for me there." The officer concluded, "Staying orders were a lot harder to swallow than marching orders."

Paul's message to Archippus is clear: "Do not walk away from the leadership assignment God has given to you." Paul's message is the sixth and final core quality of the decisive, servant, leader. It is a message of **persistence, endurance, tenacity**, and old-fashioned *stick-to-itiveness*.

Tenacity and endurance have always been attributes vital to the Christian and the Christian leader. On various occasions, God commanded Moses to persist. God kept Moses focused on his objective. Later, Isaiah underscored the rewards of patience, endurance, and persistence. "Yet those who wait for the Lord will gain strength. They will mount up with wings like eagles, they will run and not get tired, they will walk and not become weary" (Isaiah 40:30). In Hebrews 12:12, the writer asks that we follow Christ's example of endurance, *"...let us run with endurance the race that is set before us, fixing our eyes on Jesus, the author and perfector of faith, who for the joy set before Him endured the cross...."*

This endurance and clarity of purpose have also been the highlights of secular leadership. As Prime Minister of Great Britain during his country's most trying period, Sir Winston Churchill was asked to return to his high school to deliver an important speech. He received a long and glowing introduction. He arose, went to the podium, and this was his speech:

"Never, give in. Never give in. Never, never, never, never–in nothing, great or small, large or petty-never give in, except to convictions of honour and good sense. Never yield to force. Never yield to the apparently overwhelming might of the enemy." (The Best of Churchill's Speeches, 2004, p. 306)

Churchill captured in his memorable address the admonition of the Apostle Paul to Archippus, "Don't walk away from your work until God releases you from it."

I have been thinking about endurance. I am struck by how it is always needed, often painful; and it is a gracious gift.

Firstly, the **need** for endurance. Audacious tenacity — God-inspired and empowered tenacity — spiritual tenacity, if you will — is needed as a core quality of the Christian leader. We don't know why Paul was compelled to speak these words to Archippus. However, Paul's' words to his friend cause us to question why we are often tempted to *give up* on a project, an assignment, a responsibility, or a calling before genuine release comes from the Lord.

Why are we tempted to give up as Christian workers? For sure, enemies of our soul want to defeat the Christian leader. *"Our struggle is not against flesh and blood, but against the rulers, against the authorities, against the powers of the dark world and against the spiritual forces of evil in the heavenly realms"* (Ephesians 6:12).

Another reason we give up is that the problems facing us at times seem too difficult to solve. In the book, *Mastering Ministry*, Anne and Ray Ortland (1992) talk about the three time periods all problems have.

Zone A is called "Desire to Achieve" and is characterized by idealism, perhaps naiveté, and maybe apprehension.

Zone B is highlighted by the need for endurance. Zone B is called the "Desire to Quit" and is characterized by confusion and conflict when problems arise. This is the danger zone: problems need to be identified, separated, spelled out and tackled, one by one. Zone B will end in one of two ways: we will quit and abort the project, or we will *persevere* with "bull dog" tenacity, resisting the temptation to quit.

We **can** choose to believe that, even in a seemingly impossible situation, the God who has promised never to leave us or forsake us is present. We **can** choose to believe that, by the grace of God, there is a way through, over, under or around the confusing situation.

This leads us to Zone C. Zone C is called "Achievement and Growth." Christian leaders and the led characterize this zone by faith and personal satisfaction, and a sense of realism, maturity, and expectation. (p.92)

We also give up because of misconceptions regarding the Christian life, work, and ministry. These misconceptions can encourage us to give up before the job is completely finished.

"Progress is only being made
when things are running smoothly."
"The grass is greener on the other side."
"Bigger is better."
"Suffering and hardship can't be of God."
"This problem can't be solved."
"Success is gaining everyone's approval."
"Failure is final."
"I am nobody."
"Good and godly people do
not differ or make mistakes."

221

Secondly, there is the **pain** of endurance. The tendency is to "move on" when pressure builds, when we do not get our way, or the recognition we receive is not what we desire. It is painful to stay in the situation in the midst of conflict, uneasiness, misunderstanding, power struggles, conflicting, situations, and inappropriate expectations until God releases us from these assignments.

"Enduring" hardship through extraordinary times and situations requires a resolute faith in the God who has placed us in these assignments. In these "painful" experiences, we must with *conviction* believe that we remain where God has placed us until he releases us, because we serve *Him* in these painful times, not the people who sometimes inflict the pain.

We can learn much about the pain of tenacity from Ernest Shackleton and his 1914 Antarctic Expedition. Not known as a Christian leader, yet, he taught us much through example about the necessity of *endurance* in our various leadership roles (Perkins, Holtman, & Kessler, 2000).

In August 1914, Ernest Shackleton, an intrepid British explorer, boarded the ship, Endurance. He and his team of 27 men set sail for the South Atlantic. The group wanted to be the first to cross the continent of Antarctica.

Early the next year, their ship was trapped in the ice. By October 1915, still half a continent away from their intended base, the ship was crushed by ice and sank to the bottom of the ocean. In the months that followed the crew's food and water disappeared. Shackleton and his men, drifting on ice packs, were castaways in one of the most savage regions of the world. Under Shackleton's leadership, they trekked over barren, frozen ice.

More than a year after the shipwreck, Shackleton and his men were stranded on an island at the tip of Antarctica. Their food was dwindling, and there appeared little hope of rescue. Survival, Shackleton realized, depended on a bold act. Leaving most of the crew behind and with only a few of his men, he must reach a whaling outpost by crossing 800 miles of stormy seas in an open boat. Upon landing at St. George's Island, his only route to secure rescue for himself and his shipmates was still across an ominous range of glaciers and mountains that had never been crossed before. He took the chance. He had to endure. He and two others successfully reached the settlement. Amazingly, he saved his entire crew. Everyone survived. Everyone! (Perkins, Holtman, & Kessler, 2000)

Paul's journeys, as outlined in the latter book of Acts, were filled with similar experiences! Listen again to Acts 27:25, "*Keep up your courage, men, for I have faith in God that it will happen just as He told me.*"

After being in jail for two years, Paul and others were on their way to Rome. Paul's admonition to the men on board the ship was spoken in the middle of a typhoon, a shipwreck, and no food for 14 days. But, God had earlier told Paul in Jerusalem that, "*he would testify of God's grace in Rome*" (Acts 23:11). In the midst of the *pain* of getting to Rome, the jail experience, typhoon, shipwreck, and no food, Paul stated emphatically, "*...keep up your courage, men, for I have faith in God that it will happen just as he told me.*"

Ten strategies for enduring. The examples from Paul and Earnest Shackleton show that leading through extraordinary times and situations requires strategies for enduring. The following ten strategies are taken from the book, *Leading at the Edge: Leading Lessons from the Extraordinary Saga of Shackleton's Antarctic Expedition,*

(Perkins, Holtman, & Kessler, 2000).

1. **Vision and Quick Victories**: Never lose sight of the ultimate goal and focus energy on short- term objectives.

2. **Symbolism and Personal Example**: Set a personal example with visible, memorable symbols and behaviors.

3. **Optimism and Reality**: Instill optimism and self-confidence, but stay grounded in reality.

4. **Stamina:** Take care of yourself: Maintain your stamina and let go of guilt.

5. **The Team Message**: Reinforce the team message constantly: "We are one — we live or die together."

6. **Core Team Values**: Minimize status differences and insist on courtesy and mutual respect.

7. **Conflict**: Master conflict — deal with anger in small doses, engage dissidents and avoid needless power struggles.

8. **Lighten Up!** Find something to celebrate and something to laugh about.

9. **Risk**: Be willing to take the Big Risk.

10. **Tenacious Creativity**: Never give up — there's always another move.

(Perkins, Holtman, & Kessler, 2000, vii-viii)

This gift of "stick-to-itiveness"—endurance or perseverance—is not a gift we give to other people. By **no** means. Rather, the gift of tenacity is a grace gift from God to *us*...for the spiritual growth, Christian maturity, and personal development *we* experience in the midst of "staying with it" until God releases us!

On many occasions, I stated, "Leading MVNU is the greatest journey of faith I have ever experienced." In exercising tenacity—staying power—I was the greatest benefactor. In choosing to believe that God was in the midst of a process, problem, or confrontation, I grew spiritually. I matured in Christ significantly. Why? Because I had to *lead* from my knees in dependency upon the One who has called me to this assignment, believing that He would complete in my work and me exactly what He has designed!

Endurance, with contentment, is a profound gift from God to us!

God's own gift of endurance allows us to respond to God's call. Endurance enables us to "stay the course" until He releases us from an assignment! I asked a university president who had retired from his ministry several years before I did from MVNU this question: "how do you know when it is the time to retire?" His response to me was, "you will know." And he was right! Who benefits the most from the quality of endurance in the leader? Only God knows. But, for sure, we who "endure" by God's grace are blessed. Tenacity is a grace gift from God to *us*! Remember Paul's words to Archippus: *Do not walk away from the assignment God gives to you!*

Marker Six focuses on the leader as a person and examines the Christian who seeks to lead with the mind of Christ.

The qualities and values help track our integrity, assuring our words and actions are consistent. They are the indicators, the *evidence* that models for an institution the corporate and personal qualitative growth we seek to nurture in the organization and its members or employees.

We affirm these qualities in the way we live and work with others. In so doing, the individuals with whom we work in an academic community, ministry organization, or local congregation will then grow in their faith and be strengthened in their spiritual journey.

The evidence of leading, we believe, is in the qualitative growth of the led. Therefore, we desire that on a campus, an office, or on a church board, those whom we lead will mature in their faith and their walk with Christ in the midst of our life together in the organization.

This process of embedding these core qualities and core values into a ministry operation fuels the relationship between decisive leaders with a vision to serve and the led. This process engenders dialogue and communication regarding how the Christian relationship takes place between the leader and those for whom the leader is responsible.

Epilogue

We can serve as decisive leaders with integrity and grace as our testimony of holiness of heart and life continually transforms the way we live in and lead a faith community.

The people we serve should witness in us a transformed and transformative spirit reflected in the occasions of our disagreements, and in the ways we plan and process important issues. The way we preach on Sunday, live in the home, work in the community, and lead a board meeting on Tuesday evening should give evidence to an increasing "conformity to the mind of Christ" (II Cor. 3:18). Those whom we lead should see no separation between the sacred and secular in our lives. No great divide between the message we preach and the way we lead. No inconsistency. No manipulation. No disrespect. No abuse. No significant gap between our words and our deeds.

We now begin to see more clearly the means by which we "*maintain the unity of the Spirit through the bond of peace*" (Ephesians 4:3). We are learning, little by little, what it means to "imitate God...and live a life of love" (Ephesians 5:1-2), even as we lead decisively in our homes, congregations, work places, and communities.

This life-long pursuit to answer the key questions decisive leaders need to ask is a journey of maturing faith and painful encounters. It takes a lifetime to fully understand and embrace. However, the manner by which we live and lead should increasingly reflect our transformed spiritual DNA, and be profoundly evidenced in us by those who know us best.

In so walking and leading in the spirit of continuing transformation into Christlikeness, we can believe that the Master teacher and leader, Jesus the Christ, will say to us at the end of our days, "Well done, good and faithful servant." Well done.

When we come to the end of our journey, may it be said of us that we led decisively by providing something "greater than..." (John 14:12) because we were prayerful, intentional and committed disciples of Jesus! We led with clear vision, deep humility, and intense resolve. We connected the faith we profess and proclaim to the way we live and lead. What a legacy to leave behind. What a legacy!

Bibliography

"50 Awesome Quotes on Vision." *The heart of innovation.* http//www.ideachampions.com/weblogs/archive s/2015/06/50_awesome_quot_1.shtml

Augsburger, D. W. (1974). *Caring enough to confront.* Ventura, CA: Regal Books.

Bennis, W., & Biederman, P. (1997). *Organizing genius: The secrets of creative collaboration.* NY: Basic Books.

Ballie, J. (1948). *The diary of private prayer.* New York: Scribner's Sons Publishing.

Bible. K. (Ed.). (1993). *Sing to the Lord.* Kansas City, MO: Lillenas Publishing Co.

Bible. K. (Ed.). (1993). *In His Time. Sing to the Lord* (Kansas City, MO: Lillenas Publishing Company.

Blevins, D. (2015). A promised privilege (Special Edition) Holiness Today.

Blevins, D., & Maddix, M. (2010). *Discovering discipleship.* Kansas City, MO: Beacon Hill Press of Kansas City.

Bonhoeffer, D. (1954). *Life together: The classic exploration of faith in community.* New York: Harper and Row.

Bowling, J. (2000). *Grace-full leadership.* Kansas City, MO: Nazarene Publishing House.

Bridges, W. (1991). *Managing transitions: Making the most of change.* NY: Perseus Publishing.

Brown, B. (2012). *Daring greatly.* New York: Gotham Books.

Brown, B. (2015). *Rising strong.* New York: Spiegel and Grau.

Carroll, J. W. (2000). *Mainline to the future.* Louisville, KY: Westminster John Knox Press.

Carver, J. (1997). *Boards that make a difference (2nd ed).* San Francisco, CA: Jossey-Bass.

Chait, R. (2005). *Governance as leadership: Reframing the work of nonprofit boards.* Hoboken, NJ: John Wiley and Sons.

Churchill, W. (2004). *Never give in: The best of Winston Churchill's Speeches.* NY Hatchette Books.

Citrin, J., & Daum, J. (2011). *You need a leader – Now what? How to choose the best person for your organization.* NY: Crown Publishing Group.

Collins, J. (2001). *Good to great.* NY: HarperCollins.

Collins, J. (2009). *How the mighty fall.* NY: HarperCollins.

Dale, R. D. (1981). *To dream again: How to help your church come alive.* Nashville: Broadman Press.

David, F.R. (2011). *Strategic management: concepts and cases. 13th edition.* Upper Saddle River, NJ: Prentice Hall.

Day, K. (2001). *Difficult conversations: Taking risks, acting with integrity.* Washington: Alban Institute

De Pree, M. (n.d.). www.BrainyQuote.com/maxdepree.

Deurne, J. (1997). *Henri Nouwen: A restless seeking for God.* NY: Crossroads Publishing Co.

D. L. Moody quotes. (2015). Goodreads Inc. http://www.goodreads.com/author/quotes/5083 573.D_L_Moody November 3, 2015.

Fairbanks, E. L., Couchenour, J. R., & Gunter, D. M. (2012). *Best practices for effective boards*. Kansas City, MO: Beacon Hill Press of Kansas City.

Fairbanks, L. (1990). *Education for a lifestyle of service. Inaugural Address*. Mount Vernon Nazarene College. Mount Vernon, OH. www.boardserve.org/writings

Fairbanks, L., & Toler, S. (2008). *Learning to be last*. Kansas City, MO: Beacon Hill Press of Kansas City.

Friedman, E. (2007). *Leadership in the age of the quick fix: A failure of nerve*. NY: Church Publishing.

Greenleaf, R. (1977). *Servant leadership: A journey into the nature of legitimate power and greatness*. NY: Paulist Press.

Kinsler, F. R. (Ed.). (1983). *Ministry by the people*. NY: Maryknoll: Orbis Books.

Koestenbaum, P. (2002). *Leadership: The inner side of greatness - A philosophy for leaders*. San Francisco: Jossey-Bass.

Kopp, S. (1972). *If you meet the Buddha on the road, kill him* Palo Alto: Science and Behavior Books, Inc.

Kouzes, J., & Posner, B. (1995). *The leadership challenge. How to keep getting extraordinary things done in organizations (The leadership practices inventory)*. San Francisco: Jossey-Bass.

231

Kouzes, J., & Posner, B. (2002). *The leadership challenge* (3rd ed.). San Francisco: John Wiley and Sons.

Kouzes, J., & Posner, B. (2003). *Encouraging the heart.* San Francisco: Jossey Bass.

Lash. J. (1980). *Helen and teacher: The story of Helen Keller and Anne Sullivan May.* NY: Delocorte Press.

Manning, B. (2000). *Ruthless trust.* NY: Harper One.

Maxwell, J. (1993). *Developing the leader within you.* Nashville: Thomas Nelson Press.

Maxwell, L., & Dornan, J. (1997). *Becoming a person of influence.* Nashville: Thomas Nelson.

Moen, D. (1997). *Because we believe.* on Let your glory fall [Album]. www.lyrics.wekia.com

Moore, F. (Ed.). (2015). *Nazarene essentials: Who we are-What we believe. [Special edition].* Holiness Today.

Mulholland, Jr., M. R. (1993). *Invitation to a journey: A road for spiritual formation.* Downers Grove: InterVarsity Press.

National Development Institute and Clemson University. (2015 revised). *Leadership and nonprofit capacity building.* www.nationaldevelopmentinstitute.com

Nelson, A. (1994). *Broken in the right place: How God tames the soul.* Nashville: Thomas Nelson.

Nouwen, H. (1974). *Out of solitude.* Notre Dame: Ave Maria Press.

Nouwen, H. (1975). *Reaching out: Three movements of the spiritual life.* Garden City: Doubleday and Company.

Nouwen, H. (1979). *Clowning in Rome: Reflections on solitude, celibacy, prayer and contemplation.* New York: Doubleday: Image Books.

Nouwen. H. (1985a). *Bread for the journey.* CA: HarperCollins.

Nouwen, H. (1985b). *Course notes on the Gospel of John at Harvard Divinity School and at Boston College.* Found in Nouwen archives at Yale Divinity School Special Collection.

Nouwen, H. (1989). *In the name of Jesus.* NY: Crossroads Publishing Company.

Nouwen, H. (1991). *The way of the heart: Deseret spirituality and contemporary ministry.* CA: HarperCollins Paperback.

Nouwen, H.. (2009, January 12). *The spiritual work of gratitude.* [Web log post]. Retrieved from http://nouwenlegacy.blogspot.com/2009/01/spiritual-work-of-gratitude.html

Nouwen, H., McNeil, D., & Morrison D. (1983). *Compassion: A reflection on the Christian life.* New York: Image Books.

Ortland, R., & Ortland, A. (1992). *Mastering ministry.* Carol Stream: Multnomah Press.

Parrott, R. L. (Ed.). (2002). *Leadership character.* OH: Ashland Theological Seminary Press.

Perkins, D., Holtman, M., & Kessler, P. (2000). *Leading at the edge: Leadership lessons from the extraordinary expedition of Shackleton's Antarctic expedition.* NY: Amacom: American Management Association.

Pohl. C. (1999). *Making room: Recovering hospitality in Christian tradition.* Grand Rapids, MI: Eerdmans Publishing.

Powell, J. J. (1999). *Why I am afraid to tell you who I am: Insights into personal growth.* Grand Rapids: Zondervan.

Quinn, R. (1996). *Deep change.* San Francisco: Jossey-Bass.

Reed, H. (1982). *The dynamics of leadership.* Danville: The Interstate Printers and Publishers.

Robert F. Kennedy *speeches remarks at the University of Kansas, March 18, 1968. (n.d.) John F. Kennedy Presidential Library and Museum.* Retrieved on November 13, 2015 from http://www.jfklibrary.org/Research/Research-Aids/Ready-Reference/RFK-Speeches/Remarks-of-Robert-F-Kennedy-at-the-University-of-Kansas-March-18-1968.aspx

Sample, S. (2002). *The contrarian's guide to leadership.* CA: Jossey-Bass.

Satir, V. (1972). *Peoplemaking.* Palo Alto, CA: Science and Behavior Books.

Satir, V. (1976). *Making contact.* Milbrae: Celestial Arts.

Scott, S. (2004). *Fierce conversations.* NY: Berkley Publishing Group.

Shah, I. (1970). *The way of the Sufi*. NY: E.P. Dutton & Co., Inc., quoted by Sheldon B. Kopp, S., 1972). *If You Meet the Buddha on the Road, Kill Him!* Palo Alto, CA: Science and Behavior Books, Inc.

Solfield L. and Kuhn, D. (1995) *The collaborative leader*. MI: *Ava Maria Press*.

Stone, D., & Heen, S. (2014). *Thanks for the feedback*. NY: Penguin Books. Science and Behavior Books, Inc.

Trueblood, E. (1952). *Your other vocation*. NY: Harper and Row.

Wahloos, S. (1974). *Family communication*. NY: McMillian Publishing.

Weems, L. (2002). *Leadership character*. Edited by Richard Leslie Parrott. Ashland: Ashland Seminary Press.

Winer, M. (1994). *Collaboration handbook: Creating, sustaining, and enjoying the journey*. St. Paul: Amhurst H. Wilder Foundation.

Appendix A

Core Values of a Christian University ... and of Decisive and Faithful Leaders

Early in my tenure at Mount Vernon Nazarene College (now university), as enrollment expanded, I came to believe that we "owed" to the prospective students and their parents a document that outlined the core values of the institution. Perspective students were attracted to the institution because of its academic reputation, but with little knowledge of the institution, its roots, values, theological traditions or denominational relationship. I drafted the initial document, "For This We Stand: Values Underlying the Mount Vernon Nazarene University Faith Community." The draft was shared with the faculty and staff, after which the document was revised.

The following spring, the revised document was sent to all students who applied for admission. The document has been revised numerous times. The latest revision can be found at, www.mvnu.edu. Click "Information About." Click "History."

It was very apparent to me that the document reflected not only the institution but also its president, who was attempting to lead decisively and faithfully. All leaders, including parents, pastors, ministry organization directors, and college presidents need to develop their own values statement, clearly affirming the values on which they stand, and which characterize them at their best and convict them at their worst.

FOR THIS WE STAND... Values Underlying the
Mount Vernon Nazarene University Faith Community

Affirmation #1: WE LOVE GOD. Therefore, we
value and stand for...

1. *A worshiping community.*
2. *A biblical faith.*
3. *A Christlike lifestyle.*
4. *A holiness ethic.*
5. *A global mission.*
6. *A creation vision.*
7. *A Spirit-empowered devotion.*

Affirmation #2: WE RESPECT OTHERS. Therefore, we
value and stand for...

1. *A magnanimous spirit.*
2. *A servant mentality.*
3. *A trustworthy character.*
4. *A positive influence.*
5. *A courteous response.*
6. *A giving motivation.*
7. *An appreciative attitude.*

Affirmation #3: WE ARE RESPONSIBLE FOR
OURSELVES.

Therefore, we value and stand for...

1. *An inquisitive mind.*
2. *A disciplined schedule.*
3. *A modest attire.*
4. *A balanced diet.*
5. *A physical fitness commitment.*
6. *A reliable word.*
7. *A lifelong learning and growth perspective*

237

Do we always live by the values we affirm? Unfortunately, not always. For the Spirit-filled Christian, increasingly, these values — flowing from the biblical mandate to live a holy life — mark, characterize and challenge us.

Edward LeBron Fairbanks, President Emeritus,
Mount Vernon Nazarene University (retired, 2007)

Appendix B

Characteristics of Strong and Effective Governing Boards

1. Board members understand the role, purpose, and function of the board. Focus on policy formulation and mission strategy; not daily operations and implementation.

2. Board members know, communicate, and make decisions in light of the organization's mission, vision, and values. Mission, vision and values drive us.

3. Board members ask the right questions. Think questions.

4. Board members understand and embrace a board policy manual that contains the board-approved policies for effective and efficient governance of the organization. Write it down.

5. Board members communicate with each other and address conflict situations as Christians. Watch your words.

6. Board members relate to their leaders and constituency with one voice. Character counts, really counts! (Keep confidential conversations, confidential!)

7. Board members intentionally engage in mutual accountability, including systematic board development and evaluation. Board integrity matters!

8. Board members take time to process decisions, with no intentional surprises. Take time.

9. Board members embrace change and resolve to work through transitions respectively, patiently, and kindly. Yes! To missional change.

10. Board members participate in assessing the effectiveness of prior decisions. Review, revise, redirect, renew.

11. Board members are outstanding examples of providing financial oversight and giving regularly to the church, college, or organization they serve. They are role models of oversight, generosity, and stewardship.

12. Board members develop new leaders for increased responsibilities and commitment throughout the church, college, or organization. Pass it on!

How would you modify this list with additions or deletions to make these "characteristics" a mentoring outline to guide you as you work with your board? List below the top three "characteristics" or "best practices" you desire for the board with whom you work to focus during the next six to eighteen months.

For additional material, read *Best Practices for Effective Boards*, by Fairbanks, Couchenour and Gunter, Nazarene Publishing House, 2012. Available on Amazon. A DVD, "Building Better Boards", is available in English and Spanish on YouTube for use with boards in board development sessions. Search for "Fairbanks-Building Better Boards."

Appendix C

Missional Planning Template

A. Mission defines the essence of the organization. Its purpose for existence. Its reason for being.

   The Mission of the ministry organization is:

   _____

   _____

B. Vision defines the "preferred future" for the nonprofit. It is a "see" word. A future orientation. A mental image of the future.

   The Vision for the ministry organization is:

   _____

   _____

C. Values define how we intend to operate as we pursue our vision. It clarifies the parameters within which we function as an organization.

   The Values of the ministry organization are:

   _____

   _____

D. The context in which the organization functions is based on an analysis of the organization's internal strengths and weaknesses and the external opportunities and threats (SWOT Analysis).

   1. What are the ministry organization's
      a. Strengths
      b. Weaknesses

c. Opportunities

d. Threats

2. Based on the above analysis, the Priorities of the organization to which we need give our priority attention are:

_____

_____

_____

_____

3. In light of these Priorities, the Strategic Initiatives for the next three years are:

_____

_____

_____

4. The Action Plan for each Initiative includes:

a. Specific, reachable, and measurable goals:

_____

b. Timeline:

_____

c. Personnel needed and assigned:

_____

d. Budget required:

_____

e. Desired Outcomes for each of the above initiatives:

_____

_____

_____

Appendix D

Local Church Board Diagnostic

Please rate each statement as (1) strongly agree; (2) agree; (3) disagree; (4) strongly disagree:

1. The following church legal documents are up-to-date and filed in an appropriate place where board members or government agencies can quickly locate and review them, if necessary:

   - Constitution or Articles of Incorporation,
   - By-Laws,
   - NGO or not-for-profit status (in USA: 501(c)(3)),
   - Payroll documentation,
   - Insurance policies (i.e. officers, property, personal injury, etc.),
   - Other county-specific or government applicable requirements.

2. The church's mission, vision, and values are clear, understood, shared, and articulated congregation-wide.

3. The strategic planning process is understood and embraced by the congregation.

4. Board members understand their roles, functions, and expectations.

5. Board meetings are held regularly, are well attended and have detailed agendas. The board minutes are well documented.

6. The board assesses annually its performance and functions.

7. Time is designated monthly, quarterly, or yearly for board development sessions.

8. The Church has a banking account, money deposited and bills paid regularly, with clear financial reports presented at each board meeting:

9. The bookkeeping and reporting system, with the basic internal controls is reviewed periodically. The cash flow is actively managed.

10. There is a comprehensive annual budget in place, adopted by the board, and used consistently to guide financial decisions.

11. The taxes are paid, paperwork filed on time with the appropriate government agency, with an annual audit conducted.

12. There is an organization policy manual in place to guide the board in relation to employees and volunteer staff that reflects the church's mission, vision, and values.

13. There is a leader effectiveness review (or performance leadership evaluation) for the pastor and staff that is used at least biennially.

14. There is a professional development process or program in place for the pastor and staff, and this process or program is reviewed annually.

15. There is a needs assessment and program development process in place with measurable outcomes, and this plan is reviewed annually.

16. An annual report, which communicates the impact of the congregation's mission, vision, values, is provided to the congregation, and program priorities on the community served by the local church.

Organizational Capacity

Identify the top three priorities that most clearly reflect the needed priorities for the board on which you serve or lead. Why these three? What immediate steps can be taken to address these three issues?

PRIORITY #1:
PRIORITY #2:
PRIORITY #3:

Developed by BoardServe.org
www.BoardServe.org
lfairbanks@boardserve.org
Founding Director, BoardServe LLC

Appendix E

Board Evaluation Survey

Please rate each statement as (1) strongly agree; (2) agree; (3) disagree; (4) strongly disagree.

A. Board and Mission

1. Our church board ensures that our local church mission is clearly stated and understood by our board and congregation.

2. Board members know, communicate, and make decisions in light of the church's mission, vision, and values.

3. Board members regularly ask the "big" or right questions for missional strategy, fiduciary focus, effectiveness and efficiency.

B. Board/Pastor Relations

1. Board members understand the dual responsibilities of a pastor as "shepherd of the flock" and as the leader/chairperson of the local church board.

2. The Board works closely with the pastor in shaping and evaluating policies for fiduciary oversight, developing strategic plans and programs, providing policy and program reviews, and in the shaping of the "big-picture" issues.

3. There is a climate of mutual trust and support between the Board and the pastor.

4. The Board openly champions the current direction for the local church and vision as advocated by the pastor and affirmed by the Board.

5. The pastor keeps the Board informed on strategic issues facing the local church.

C. Member to Member Relations

1. Members of the Board communicate with each other and address conflict situations as Christians.

2. Board members vigorously discuss policy options in the Board meetings; yet communicate a united voice to the congregation once a decision has been made.

3. Discussion among members in board meetings focuses on missional, policy and strategic questions, not on personality and personal differences.

4. Board members nurture strong personal relationships within the board.

5. Confidential discussions in board meetings remain confidential following the board meetings.

D. The Board Agenda

1. The board agenda reflects a clear understanding of the role, purpose, and function of the board.

2. The board has a detailed agenda established for each meeting, and the agenda is received in a timely manner.

3. Meeting agendas focus on policy issues and missional planning.

4. The board agenda includes all necessary supporting information.

E. **The Organization of the Board**

1. The Board is organized such that it is effective, garners high-level participation, and engenders confidence from the constituencies.

2. The Board is composed of a sufficient cross section of strong and mature members to allow it to significantly develop the local church.

3. The Board has approved a property master plan and monitors the maintenance programs sufficiently to be assured that they are not deferred to the detriment of the local church.

4. The Board designates specific times yearly for prayer and fasting.

5. The committee structure facilitate the work of the Board efficiently:

F. **The Functioning of the Board**

1. The Board seeks feedback from and communicates effectively with the congregation regarding issues and actions of the Board.

2. The Board takes leadership responsibility for the financial management of the local church, and fund-raising, if necessary, to assure that sufficient resources are available to fulfill the mission of the congregation.

3. The Board periodically evaluates its own functioning and effectiveness as a Board.

4. The Board maintains and posts appropriate written minutes of the meetings, and has a Board Handbook for its policies.

5. The Board invites non-board members, as appropriate, to assist the Board in areas where additional competencies are needed by the Board to understand and address critical issues.

G. Nuts and Bolts

1. Prayer is an important component of Board meetings.

2. Members of the Board are elected following Manual guidelines.

3. An appropriate orientation session is provided yearly for new members?

4. Board meetings are of sufficient duration and frequency to appropriately do the business of the Board.

H. Summary

Use additional space to answer these questions or to comment on the survey.

1. The major strengths of our Board are:

_____

_____

2. Three Board DEVELOPMENT issues we should focus on during the next 18 months are:

_____

_____

_____

Prepared by Edward LeBron Fairbanks,
BoardServe LLC founder and director,
www.boardserve.org
lfairbanks@boardserve.org

Contact the author of the questionnaire at the address above for additional information. This questionnaire may be reproduced or modified, as necessary, with written permission from BoardServe.org

Appendix F

Leader Effectiveness Review

Date:

Board Appointed Review Team: (names deleted)

The following review process has been initiated in an attempt to be a faithful steward of the leadership assignment given to the principal of the College on which Board you serve. Fundamental to the nature of this review process is mutual dialogue between the principal and Board of Trustees to whom the Principal reports. This is a critical component of the review process. The Board has appointed a subcommittee to lead this review, as the Board prepares for a renewal vote of the College principal for another four years.

The review has three sections to be completed by the Principal prior to the official Review Committee Meeting (RCM). Section two is also to be completed by the Board-appointed committee members and College faculty and staff, full- and part-time. The "Competency Grid" attached to section two may be used by the Review Committee chairperson to facilitate the "Gap Analysis" discussion stemming from this section.

The date for the RCM is set for 8:00am, on Saturday,_____, 201__. The RCM will include the Board Review Committee and the College Principal. The Board chair will convene a meeting of the Board Review Committee no later than two weeks following the review to shape the Review Committee report to the Board and a recommendation regarding the renewal vote at the annual meeting of the College board.

Reflections/Projections (to be answered by the Principal prior to the RCM).

1. Has your sense of calling and personal ministry been fulfilled through your leadership endeavors? If not, why? If so, how? Do you feel affirmed as a valuable asset? If not, why? If so, how?

2. How does your specific assignment as Principal support the overarching mission and vision of the College you serve? Provide some examples.

3. Do you feel you have an adequate position description approved by the Board? How could the written expectations be improved and strengthened?

4. In what ways have you developed and enhanced your job knowledge and performance? Have adequate opportunities been provided both for training and for personal growth since your last review/evaluation? Please give examples.

5. What specific tasks or accomplishments during the past four years best express your commitment to quality service and servant leadership to the College's multiple constituents such as administrative decision-making, curriculum relevancy, leadership development, evangelism, discipleship training, fiscal management, team building and vision casting? How have your gifts and talents been most effectively used?

6. In what ways have your initiatives contributed to the numerical growth and spiritual development of the institution you serve? What additional resources might assist you as your strive to strengthen the College?

7. How can the climate of collaboration within the College and with other institutions (colleges/universities, denominations, ministry organizations, etc.) be enhanced?

8. In what ways can the Board of Trustees support you to lead more effectively?

9. What are your three top college challenges for the next year? The next four years? What short-term and long-term goals have you established for your assignment in light of these challenges? How will you know when your goals have been reached?

10. Are your short-term and long-term goals aligned with the College's strategic plan? Please give examples.

Peer Evaluation of the Principal and Gap Analysis of Responses

To be completed by the college Principal, and anonymously by the College faculty and staff, full- and part-time, and the Board Review Committee members. The Evaluation will be distributed to the faculty and staff with an explanatory note. The evaluation section will be coordinated by the Board chair, who also will analyze the results of the evaluation, including the responses of the Principal, in preparation for the Review Committee Meeting (RCM).

Instructions: Please circle the number for each statement that most characterizes the Principal, from:
1 (never); 2 (seldom); 3 (occasionally); 4 (often); 5 (always).

1. The Principal uses words that serve to encourage others.

   1   2   3   4   5

2. The Principal gives gratitude to God and others as a fundamental lifestyle.

   1   2   3   4   5

3. People feel understood when communicating with the Principal.

   1   2   3   4   5

4. Extending and requesting forgiveness is a core communication component of the Principal.

   1   2   3   4   5

5. A clear "vision" is embodied, embraced, and articulated by the Principal.

   1   2   3   4   5

6. The public prayers of the Principal reflect a desire for personal change.

   1   2   3   4   5

7. Caring for personal and professional growth of colleagues is important to the Principal.

   1   2   3   4   5

8. Words spoken are culturally sensitive and consistent with actions taken by the Principal.

   1   2   3   4   5

9. Comparison to others (regions, districts, finances, talents, etc.) by the Principal is minimal.

   1   2   3   4   5

10. Honest and intense differences with others are accepted by the Principal.

    1   2   3   4   5

11. The Principal does not harbor resentment and bitterness toward others.

    1   2   3   4   5

12. Prayer for colleagues, staff, and the ministry is often and evident.

    1   2   3   4   5

13. Responsibility for decisive decision-making, as needed and administrative oversight, does not paralyze the Principal.

    1   2   3   4   5

14. The primary focus of the Principal is on plans and programs that unite, not divide.

    1   2   3   4   5

15. Colleagues feel blessed and affirmed in conversations and meetings with the Principal.

    1   2   3   4   5

16. The Principal brings out the "best" in others.

    1   2   3   4   5

17. People feel valued when discussing issues with the Principal.

    1   2   3   4   5

18. Extending forgiveness is convictional to the Principal.

    1   2   3   4   5

19. The Principal leads decisively and with administrative skill in the midst of complex and difficult situations.

   1   2   3   4   5

20. The Principal values people, not power and position.

   1   2   3   4   5

21. The Principal leads with the conviction that some issues are only resolved through prayer and total dependence on God.

   1   2   3   4   5

In looking towards the future, please rank in order of priority (1 = least important; 7 = most important) the leadership skills that should be nurtured during the next four years. The ranking is not an evaluation of past performance. Rather, it is a projection for the next four years.

- ☐ Affirming and Encouraging skills
- ☐ Asking and Listening skills
- ☐ Conceptual and Analytical skills
- ☐ Financial Management, Budget and Capital Fund Development skills
- ☐ "Strengths" Discernment and Delegation skills
- ☐ Networking and Communication skills
- ☐ Timing and Decision Making skills

Summary (to be completed in writing by the Principal prior to the RCM).

_____

_____

256

Provide a summary of your leadership strengths and how these are most effectively utilized in your ministry assignment as a school leader?

_____

_____

Provide a summary of your leadership limitations and how you plan to address these during the next four years?

_____

_____

Provide a summary of your College Action Plan (AP) for the next four years.

_____

_____

Recommendation:
The Board Review Team will meet two weeks following the review to shape a report and recommendation to the full Board.

Developed by Edward LeBron Fairbanks
Used by permission of BoardServe.org

Appendix G

Permission to Reprint from Jimmy LaRose

Please allow this email to serve as my written express permission for E. LeBron Fairbanks to use any material originated by Jimmy LaRose as he deems fit.

The attached document has been updates with three significant changes.

www.MajorGiftsRampUp.com
www.NonprofitConferences.org
www.ConsultingCertification.org
www.JimmyLaRose.com

Warmly,

Jimmy

P.O. Box 1840
Lexington, SC 29071
Office: 803-808-5084
Fax: 803-808-0537
Mobile: 803-477-6242
Email: jimmy@jimmylarose.com

Appendix H

Template
Board Policy Manual or
Organizational Handbook

The Board Standing Policy Manual contains all the standards or on-going policies adopted by the Board of Governance for the organization, congregation or institution.

Reasons for Adoption:

1. Efficiency of having ALL ongoing Board policies in one place;

2. Ability to quickly orient new board members to current policies;

3. Elimination of redundancy or conflicting policies over time;

4. Ease of reviewing current policy when considering new issues;

5. Provides an approach to governance that sister organizations, institutions, or congregations may use.

The Board Policy Manual or Organizational Handbook usually contains at least four brief sections in addition to the Introduction:

I. **Introduction.** This section of the manual or handbook includes the by-laws and the Articles of Incorporation, and other legal or government documents required to be up to date for the organization.

II. **Organizational ends toward which we are working - mission, vision and values**. This section defines why we exist, what we intend to contribute to those for whom we exist, and the priorities we assign to the benefits we provide to them.

III. **Board governance process**. This section defines how the Board will go about doing its work go governing the organization.

IV. **Board/Pastor, Executive Director or President Relationship**. This section defines how the Board will delegate authority and responsibility to the president.

V. **Executive Parameters**. This section defines the parameters/limitations within which the executive director, pastor, or president will work in accomplishing his/her assigned tasks.

*Adopted from the writings of John Carver on Board Governance. See Carver, John. Boards That Make A Difference. Second Edition. (San Francisco: Jossey-Bass, 1997. See also Chait, Richard P. Govern. Governance as Leadership. Hoboken: Boardsource, Inc.

The Author

Edward LeBron Fairbanks founded and has served as the director of BoardServe LLC since 2011. The consulting service nurtures "transformed and transformative" governing boards of Christian organizations, including universities and seminaries, not-for-profit organizations, and local churches.

He retired in October 2011 as the education commissioner for the Church of the Nazarene. In this assignment, he served as the administrator of the International Board of Education (IBOE), a consortium of 52 denominational universities, colleges, and seminaries on campuses and learning centers in 120 nations. He worked closely with the 13-member IBOE in strengthening the Nazarene higher education institutions worldwide.

Dr. Fairbanks co-authored the leadership text, *Learning to be Last: Leadership for Congregational Transformation* in 2008 and *Best Practices for Effective Boards* in 2012. He created the teaching video, *Building Better Boards: A Conversation*, produced in 2012, and available in English and Spanish. In addition, he has written numerous books and articles, including the ministerial course of study text, *Leading the People of God: Servant Leadership for a Servant Community*.

Dr. Fairbanks earned his bachelor's degree at Trevecca Nazarene University. He also earned three master's degrees — M.A. from Scarritt College, M.Div. from the Nazarene Theological Seminary, and M.Th. from Princeton Theological Seminary.

He was designated a Fellow in Pastoral Leadership Education by Princeton Theological Seminary and earned the Doctor of Ministry degree from Nazarene Theological Seminary. Dr. Fairbanks completed the summer program at the Harvard University Institute of Educational Management and was a Research Fellow at Yale University Divinity School.

Dr. Fairbanks became Academic Dean in 1978 for the European Nazarene College near Schaffhausen, Switzerland. In 1984, he was elected President of the Asia-Pacific Nazarene Theological Seminary in Manila, Philippines, where he served until accepting the presidency of Mount Vernon Nazarene University in Mount Vernon, Ohio, in July 1989. He served MVNU as university president for 18 years, retiring in 2007.

In addition to his BoardServe consulting service, Dr. Fairbanks served in interim leadership roles in Brisbane, Australia, and Tampa, Florida. He taught leadership classes in the past three years in Manila, Philippines; Gelnhausen, Germany; Lisbon, Portugal; and Yangon, Myanmar (Burma).

He and his wife, Anne, have been married for over 50 years and have one son, Stephen. Dr. Fairbanks can be contacted at lfairbanks@boardserve.org. His blog/website address is: www.boardserve.org.

12443250R00155

Made in the USA
Middletown, DE
23 November 2018